Bridges of the Spirit

Bridges of the Spirit

Maureen Edwards

First published in Great Britain 1994
Society for Promoting Christian Knowledge
Holy Trinity Church
Marylebone Road
London NW1 4DU

British Library Cataloguing-in-Publication Data

A catalogue record for this book is available
from the British Library

ISBN 0-281-04770-7

Typeset by Pioneer Associates, Perthshire
Printed in Great Britain by
Biddles Ltd., Guildford and King's Lynn

The presence of somebody from another country is a clear expression of the one mission that God has called us to. . .

Farai Chirisa, former President of the Methodist Church Zimbabwe

Let our partnership be seen to be real. The Church of God is universal and there would be no other way of expressing this than the sharing of personnel.

The Bishop of Central Zambia, from a letter to UPSG

Contents

Preface

The idea for this book came to me during the years when I worked for the Methodist Church Overseas Division in London and received many letters from both adults and young people asking for something which tells the stories of today's missionaries. But because I believe that mission is not limited to those who are sent by mission agencies, the stories include some who would not call themselves 'missionaries'. They are stories about Christians led by the Spirit to cross over and work with people of other cultures. And today, that can even be done in our own community! The nature of their work and the challenges they make to us are extremely varied.

Most stories are based on live interviews and a few on letters and other documents. I would like to express my appreciation to individuals, families and the staff of mission agencies who have given me their time and hospitality to answer my questions, checked manuscripts and encouraged and supported the project.

I hope this book will be used
- to enthuse those who read it with a wider vision of what it means to be members of the World Church and become engaged in God's mission, for that is a task for all who follow Christ;
- to help those who may be thinking about going to work in another part of the world;
- to update our understanding of new developments in mission;
- to provoke Christians to take up new issues and challenges and, in a spirit of openness, to discover how the

Spirit is leading us all to a deeper understanding of one another, that we may work together for justice and peace for all God's creation.

To enable both personal and group discussion on the issues raised, some biblical reflections are added with suggestions for leaders of house groups.

1

Come over and help us

Meeting people face to face and learning about their lives,
their hopes and fears is enriching to all who take part. It
helps to foster a sense of interdependence and involvement together in the body of Christ.

Council for World Mission

Nyaminyami, an arid area of Northern Zimbabwe, had
become a refuge for the Batonga people, whose homes on
the banks of the Zambezi were flooded when the Kariba
Dam was built. Apart from a few Christians here and there
and one small Methodist congregation, there was, until the
1980s, no church of any kind. During a long drought,
Morris Maswanise, a Methodist minister, began to visit the
area, making sure people had enough food. Having won
their confidence, he wrote to the Methodist headquarters in
Harare sharing with his church leaders his idea to build a
church in that area and set up a mobile clinic offering
primary health care. About the same time, the Methodist
Church Overseas Division in London (MCOD) wrote to the
Methodist Church Zimbabwe (MCZ) asking if there were any
ventures in outreach in which they could be involved as
partners. It seemed like the prompting of the Spirit and a
response to the 'call in the night': 'Come over and help us.'

Representatives of both churches visited the area together
and pledged themselves to a 'new initiative' in mission.
Morris Maswanise was stationed there as minister and
MCOD provided a grant for the manse and a mobile clinic,
while the MCZ covered his stipend and travelling expenses.
In January 1988 Deina Smith, a nurse from Manchester, was

1

sent to work with Morris Maswanise, to run the clinic and train local midwives. Their main task is pastoral and evangelistic: to share the life of the people, their hopes and deprivation, proclaiming together the wholeness of the gospel.

This sharing of personnel happens in a variety of ways, officially through mission agencies and unofficially by those who feel prompted to go and work in another part of the world or across cultures in their own community. The movement of the Spirit is not confined by church organization! Christians in the West are invited to use their skills as priests, teachers, doctors, health workers, administrators, and other less usual forms of service. Andy Bowman, for example, with a degree in interior design, was designated by USPG to work with an ecumenical project in Chile which builds low-cost housing in Concepcion.

An interesting example of someone who would not be called a missionary is Greg Newton, a youth worker from the Redhill and Reigate YMCA, who was sent by the Council of Churches for Britain and Ireland (CCBI) to China for six months to study at the University of Shanghai and to teach English to young adults in the YM/YWCA. At the time of writing, having raised the money for his travel expenses, he has just arrived, keen 'to grow in understanding of the world'. Already he is aware of the experience of many who discovered Christ in the lives of committed YMCA staff without a word being spoken about their faith (evangelism is still forbidden in China), and that there are other ways of building the Kingdom. Greg's placement is a new initiative, another step in the process of building relationships with the church and Christian organizations in China. The CCBI's approach is based on respect for China's principles of self-government, self-support, and self-propagation; and this placement is intended to encourage growth towards these goals.

The qualifications for those who cross over to work with people of other cultures are not only specialized ones. Like Abraham, they go out not knowing where they will be led or what new challenges they will have to face. They need flexibility: having been sent to do one job, they may find, on arrival, that they are expected to do something very different. They need an openness to learn from those with whom they work, a sense of humour, a readiness to get their hands dirty and learn the language, and an inner strength. Many have to be able to cope in situations of political insecurity and violence. And, being expatriates, mere observers on the sidelines of mostly one-party states, they are not free to express an opinion.

Despite the welcome given by church leaders, they may have to wrestle with difficult questions. Stephen Barton, who went to Bangladesh and whose story is told later, was acutely aware of the popular Bangladeshi image of the church as 'a foreign organization' and had the uncomfortable feeling that his presence as a white missionary seemed to reinforce this image. Roman Catholic and Church of Bangladesh missionaries actually go at the invitation of and to work under the authority of indigenous leadership. But hundreds of other missionaries are sent by other (mostly American based) mission agencies without consultation with local Christians. Their lack of sensitivity to local expectations does much to reinforce the prejudice of many Bangladeshis.

Stephen Barton points out that, like other partner churches round the world, the Church of Bangladesh receives financial aid from a number of agencies in Europe, North America, Japan, and Australia, and this money is channelled into impressive development projects. While these are not in themselves controlled by the donors, the church is nevertheless dependent on them and is itself ostensibly a large institution handling huge sums of foreign money, so that government officials suspect Christians of running projects to gain converts. Christians are a small minority in Bangladesh, just 0.3% of the population. They feel vulnerable. In Bangladesh, Christians are not threatened but nationals and expatriates alike struggle with these subtle pressures.

Many of those who go from the 'one-third world' to the

'two-thirds world' are invited to share a gift or skill to meet a need, but they return realizing how much western society has to learn from the rest of the world: from other peoples' sense of community, their traditions of friendliness and open hospitality, their lack of wastefulness, a natural sensitivity to the presence of God in the whole of life, a different concept of time. In the same way, in supposedly 'developed' countries we are beginning to realize our desperate need of the spiritual gifts Christians from other parts of the world have to share with us and which would bring us wholeness, and we have begun to say, 'Come over and help us.'

Through the growing number of teams and individuals invited to Britain to visit and serve with local churches, the lives of more and more Christians are touched by people of other cultures and, through living in an increasingly multiracial society, by people of other faiths. The Spirit, who moves ahead of us setting up bridges, beckons the whole church, and indeed the whole world, to cross, to meet, to listen, to learn, and to be changed. Yet for most, 'change' is the most threatening factor. It all depends on what you mean by 'conversion'. The story of the conversion of Cornelius in Acts 10 focuses sharply on the conversion of Peter from a traditionalism that defended the *status quo* to a faith that became more open to the leading of the Spirit to embrace people of other cultures. We will not really share effectively in God's mission to 'reconcile all things to himself' unless we see conversion not as a once for all time experience, but as an ongoing process of *'metanoia'*—a complete change of direction. Mission can only take place where there is repentance and a shedding of power and privilege.

This means taking one another seriously. Even now, encounters with Christians in other parts of the world are too easily dismissed at the end of a church meeting with a kindly expression of thanks, instead of struggling with a change of attitude, policy and action, because the gospel Jesus proclaimed, and which the poor receive gladly, makes uncomfortable challenges about divesting ourselves of power. This is the challenge that comes, for instance, from

Christians in Latin America, who have found a new, more participative way of being the church and are themselves actively involved, in the name of Christ, in the struggle for social justice and equality.

It is vital therefore that all western Christians—whose traditional role has been to give, initiate, and lead—become more critical of their attitude to the rest of the world and learn to listen and receive. But how many Christians will admit that they need to learn from other cultures? In 1985, during a visit to the Caribbean, Allan Kirton, a staff member of the Caribbean Conference of Churches, asked me, 'Can a church that has traditionally been in the position of giving, receive? Is it able to receive?' Another Caribbean minister, Claude Cadogan, told me of an occasion when an American colleague, whom he was meeting at a consultation in the US, asked him to bring a jar of Blue Mountain coffee from Jamaica. When the American asked how much it cost and Claude Cadogan replied that it was gift, the American insisted on paying him five dollars and, on the next day, gave him an extra forty-seven cents to make up his payment to the price marked on the bottle! When they were due to meet again, he asked him to bring another jar of coffee, but this time Claude Cadogan refused. 'He could not see himself receiving gifts from me,' he said. 'He had to learn that from our side of the world, we can offer gifts as well as receive them. We are stressing mutuality as distinct from the old-time type of mission which came down a one-way street from mother churches. We were brought up to think of receiving, being helped, taught, and guided. We were made to think we were poor and unable to offer what would be of value to others. Yet we realize that we are falling short of our own fulfilment unless, in turn, we are able to give and offer service. And those with whom we come into contact, and with whom we work, have got to learn how to receive.'

During that same visit, I met a young Samoan minister, Samuel Faiaia, serving in the north of Jamaica. He took me with him to visit a very old lady aged one hundred and two.

As we approached her house, he talked of her great faith and love of her Lord. 'When I visit her, she strengthens me more than I can help her,' he said. As I sat with them and they ministered to one another, they ministered to me as well. It was a precious experience, the world church in microcosm—mission, not just between different cultures and representatives from geographically separated areas of the world, but transcending all differences of age and social grouping.

2

Responding to the invitation

Overcoming stigmas

ROS COLWILL — Britain to Nigeria

Ros Colwill, a Roman Catholic, always wanted to work with those who are rejected by their families and society. 'Christ has always been for me', she says, 'the person who came to set the captives free, to open the prison doors, to feed the hungry and care for the sick. That's been with me since I was a child.'

While at university, Ros worked as a volunteer with the Cyrenian Community in Swansea. The Cyrenians help single homeless people, gathering them together in small houses of eight or ten residents, each with two workers. In 1973 she worked for a time with Mother Teresa in the original House for Dying Destitutes in Calcutta, caring for those whom no one else would touch. But not everyone died and, at that time, there were no plans or policies for the rehabilitation of those who recovered. Ros was acutely aware of this. She then worked for four months with the probation service in Jamaica, and for a year with deprived children with the Church of Bangladesh. On her return to England in 1977, she worked full-time for three years with the Cyrenians in West London, but wanted to go overseas again. She began looking at the options and making enquiries. A friend showed her a Christians Abroad publication advertising for someone to work at Uzuakoli, a leprosy settlement in southern Nigeria. The settlement, which belonged to the Methodist Church Nigeria, had been badly destroyed by civil war and little had been done to restore it. Here was the kind of challenge she was looking for—to go in and help rebuild it with 'a new face'. Since leprosy could now be cured, the emphasis would be on rehabilitation.

Ros first went to Nigeria in March 1981 and helped the community at Uzuakoli to rebuild their homes and develop a variety of workshops for rehabilitation and vocational skills: brick-making, weaving, sewing, shoemaking, farming and many other activities, all based on the use of local materials. It was an experience of resurrection for the community. And at the centre of it still is a church, its pattern of worship integrating the everyday life of the settlement and symbolizing the presence of Christ in their midst.

As her time there drew to a close, Ros began to notice the growing number of vagrant psychotics on the streets, naked, malnourished, covered in sores, often chained and disfigured and—as a result of years of living rough—hostile and withdrawn. The number seemed to grow daily and no one cared, Church or State, so Ros asked the Methodist Church Nigeria if something could be done for them. At first she met considerable resistance. The stigma of mental illness was every bit as great as that for leprosy. No one believed they could be brought from the streets into a community. The vision which Ros shared with the church was of a place of belonging, into which these bruised, ostracized men and women could be gathered, loved, and healed so that they could take up the reins of life again. 'God is a descending God,' she said, and went on to remind us all that Jesus, who declined to wield influence in an 'upwardly mobile' society, opted for what was small, hidden, and poor.

First, Ros spent three months travelling around the country to meet professors of psychiatry, traditional healers, people with ideas in the field of mental health, and was greatly influenced by all that she learnt of the work of Jean Vanier and L'Arche communities for the mentally ill and handicapped worldwide. She was also involved in endless negotiations over the purchase of land: seven months of meetings at the chief's home, chewing kola nuts and drinking palm wine. In African tradition, everyone must be permitted to speak and share in decision-making. Finally a feast in the palace of the Eze (traditional ruler) symbolized a new relationship between church and society. The land was paid for with a goat, eight yams, two kegs of palm wine, a bag of kola nuts, a bottle of Schnapps and a crate of mineral drinks!

The first task for Ros and her small band of helpers—four cured leprosy sufferers from Uzuakoli and one little adopted boy—was to begin to transform a vast expanse of bush into a community of homes with a herbal farm, orchards, fish-ponds, trees, and gardens. Houses, built of local bricks and with tiled roofs, form a traditional African circle, and in the heart of the circle is a circular chapel. There is a kitchen, a dining room (even the tables are round), a community centre and two large buildings for eight open-plan workshops. In Igbo, they called this village 'Amaudo'—'Village of peace'. Initially, this community was an act of faith with no financial backing, but grants have come from many quarters both inside and outside Nigeria.

At first, they collected small numbers of the mentally ill and destitute from the streets and brought them in as buildings were completed. In just six months there were thirty mentally ill people with fifteen helpers and, since February 1992, when the last building was completed, there has been a strong community of eighty-seven, including seven children of destitutes and fifteen full-time workers, to ensure that one-to-one help can be given when needed. There are no security gates, locks, or fences. After three weeks, patients are stabilized by drugs which remove the distressing effects of the hallucinations and delusions that often make them frightened. The approach is holistic, using prayer, drugs, and large amounts of tender loving care. For six months Ros worked closely with the local traditional healer, listening to him talk of his skills, his understanding of mental illness, the use of herbs, roots, and barks of trees, and learning from the African mind to divine the source of sickness. 'We don't know all the answers', she says, 'and this is exciting because it makes you more open to learn.'

In illness, the African seeks to understand the imbalances between ourselves and the environment and to explore how we may have offended the community or an individual. Only by offering a sacrifice can the imbalance be put right. A cock is killed and the blood poured over the patient's head. By this action, health is restored. Many African Christians, conditioned by former colonial and missionary attitudes, are troubled by actions like this: they seem to compromise with evil. But until the patient receives the action he expects, he won't recover, or, if he does, the madness will come back. Does it work like a placebo? Or is it a matter of respecting other time-honoured ways of healing?

Vital in the community is Amaudo's full-time chaplain, Innocent Ekeke. From the beginning, daily prayers for everyone in the community have been a focal point of Amaudo's life in which broken people are made whole by the power of the gospel.

Workshops in groups of five to seven include tailoring, bag-making, jewellery, hairdressing, typing, shoemaking, agriculture, tile-making, and pottery. This three-hour period of concentration in the mornings is a chance to work together in small groups, to discover mutual support, to learn a skill, to achieve something. Through its small industries and farming, Amaudo should become more or less self-supporting. The pottery is purely income generating and should provide fifteen per cent of its income. And there are plans for the development of a textile industry, being worked out with the help of a link-group in Bristol, to make fashionable African prints. Many people are involved in farming to provide meat, oil, and fresh vegetables for the community. Evening literacy classes are given by teachers from the village. This is all part of their recovery, and so are the sports activities which help in building relationships. Regular house meetings, in each unit of eight residents with their house parent, encourage them to share in the organization of community life and decisions about future developments. Once a month, the community meeting (two representatives from each house meeting and the workers' representatives) plans the ongoing life of the community.

Neighbours in surrounding villages can hardly believe the difference between the state of the original mentally ill destitute and what he or she becomes at Amaudo. One example is a young man called Fred, whom Ros first heard about because he had attacked a VSO volunteer working in the same State. He was to be seen with his hands and feet chained, shuffling along the road, naked, angry, and often violent, attacking houses and passers-by. He had been ill for nine years, treated mostly by native doctors. When his father died, he became head of the family, but because he was mentally ill, his mother allowed a rather rapacious uncle to get his hands on the property and signed everything over to him. That only made Fred more distressed. At Amaudo, he made a remarkable recovery. It was clear that he had had a good education and he was encouraged to use it. He may now be found teaching in the Amaudo Nursery School, very much at peace with himself and the world. At the time of writing, he is able to go home on visits, learning how to handle his feelings and relationship with his family.

Amaudo aims not to institutionalize, but to enable residents to recover and return to their homes. The patient's future is not in Amaudo but the wider community. Residents take part in whatever is going on around them, especially cultural and religious festivals, and invite neighbours to come and share their times of worship. They have a band of quite a professional standard which is hired out most weekends for special events. There is a strong relationship between Amaudo and the Eze. Amaudo is becoming an integral part of village life and this in turn is drawing attention to the once isolated Itumbauzo. The nursery school is sited in the village and provides a higher quality education than state primary schools. Children from Amaudo attend school with the village children. Itumbauzo, a rural community of subsistence farmers on the borders of Imo State, is isolated from the mainstream of

Nigerian life. The advent of Amaudo is beginning to make a difference to the whole neighbourhood.

Everyone who is discharged from Amaudo is given a small grant to start a trade and buy tools. Days when an individual or group is discharged are times of celebration with a special service in the chapel. On one such occasion Ros wrote: 'To our sheer joy more than eighty relatives came to the service to carry her home, including her husband and her five children. This woman had been destitute for eight years on the streets. It was such a moving occasion, (with) singing and dancing.' Another letter describes a discharge service for four women. One is now selling rice and beans in her village; the second is apprenticed to a seamstress; the third is selling crayfish and the fourth, who is deaf and too retarded to be able to work, is reunited with her husband. She had been lost and thought dead for three years: his joy at receiving her back was deeply moving. In the last week of each month, workers visit all the discharged in their homes, to give injections (maintenance doses of drugs) and provide counselling for them and their families.

A new site in Ntalakwu, the next village, has been donated by the village for the long-term care of the few chronic cases, especially the mentally handicapped, who have no one to care for them at home. This frees accommodation at Amaudo for more vagrant psychotics.

Ros believes it is not enough to offer cures. In addition people must work to change government policies for the mentally ill and for a change of attitude in society. Amaudo, in collaboration with the state government, has set up a community psychiatric programme, so that mentally ill people do not end up destitute on the streets. Thirteen psychiatric nurses, so far, are posted in primary health care centres. For the first time in the Abia State of Nigeria, the mentally ill can go to a clinic in their own area and receive drugs at a minimal charge. The Federal Government sees this as a pilot project. If it works, they can learn from it and implement similar programmes in other States. All this is a tremendous achievement against the background of political transition, and inflation which reached one hundred per cent in 1993.

Now that Amaudo is 'on its feet' Ros is looking for new challenges. One is to do something for mentally ill prisoners, often put into state prisons by uncaring relatives on false charges. Not far from Amaudo is a prison that has recently been renovated and improved, apart from the psychiatric wing. There, a hundred or so men are left naked, weak, hungry, with no soap, suffering severe skin disorders and dying at the rate of two a week. No one goes near them. Ros has already approached the chief judge of the state who agreed to allow her to begin taking a few at a time into Amaudo. And, having got a foothold in the prison, she hopes to encourage other improvements there.

Ros recognizes that to continue working in Nigeria for a longer period of time will make it possible to effect real change in the lives of people who might not otherwise be noticed, to move into other areas of stigmatization, to work towards new methods of caring and new attitudes in government and society. Ros cannot see herself coming back to live in Britain. In Nigeria, she is doing just what she enjoys and the longer she lives away from home, the more alienated she feels from western values and lifestyle. She is taking out Nigerian citizenship to get around that government's clampdown on 'evangelizing missionaries'. It is becoming increasingly difficult to get missionary personnel into Nigeria.

As a Roman Catholic, Ros had never been inside a Methodist church before! So it has been exciting, a tremendous privilege, to be part of the executive body of Methodist Church Nigeria and to be fully involved in its organization and development. That would be impossible in the Roman Catholic Church. Working with Methodist Church Nigeria has been affirming and strengthening for her faith. Sometimes traditional Catholic friends have commented that she ought to be at Mass on Sundays rather than worshipping at Amaudo. She replies that she can't feel the guilt of this any more than Jesus did when he performed miracles of healing on the Sabbath. The Roman Catholic Church will always be her spiritual home, the place where her roots are, but she has learnt in Nigeria that denominationalism is irrelevant.

Participation is the key

DAVID SHARLAND — Britain to Zaire

David and Jesse had been distributing blankets and hoes to Sudanese refugees all day in NE Zaire. Witnessing suffering is never easy and they were drained of emotion. Then Jesse noticed a young boy of about twelve and brought him to David. The boy's parents had been shot in the Sudan and he had fled to Zaire. Because he had no family, he had not been counted in any of the surveys. How easy it was to pass by the most needy, they reflected.

Jesse, a fine preacher, is a man of great compassion and sensitivity. He and David have worked together for a few years now, travelling from Aru out to the villages and refugee camps on their four-wheel drive motor bike. Jesse has had a hard life. Born in Zaire, he was partly educated in Uganda until he and his family fled from the atrocities of Idi Amin back into NE Zaire. Despite two personal tragedies—both his first wife and oldest son were poisoned because of bitterness and rivalry in the village—he helped and encouraged his people to plant trees and fruit and to build a dispensary. Then David Sharland, a CMS missionary, asked him to come down to Aru to work with him. Jesse has a real concern for others and this is a good partnership.

There are 70,000 refugees in the area. There is not much the Church of Zaire can do to help such a vast number, but Tear Fund has provided blankets, saucepans, hoes, and other essentials. In view of the deteriorating situation in the Sudan, they are likely to be there for a few years, and David and Jesse are organizing more long-term help. First, they are helping people to know their rights—especially in regard to land—and are encouraging them to set up farming co-operatives, so that in time they can become self-supporting. Some refugees are being trained in carpentry so that in turn they can train another eight apprentices. There is always a need for furniture, and tools can be provided. Craft work-shops with sewing-machines will be provided for women's groups. It is good to see these groups develop an interest in Bible study and this often finds expression in practical and mutual support.

Although David Sharland is no educationalist, he was pressed to open two schools for refugee children. He agreed only on condition that the parents provided the labour and became involved in making it work. Now there are 600 children in each school. Refugee teachers, who work for just £3 per month, are provided with blackboards, textbooks, exercise books, and pencils. Some classrooms have benches, but many children have to sit on the floor. The transfor-mation is unbelievable. A rabble of noisy, frustrated children have become two disciplined school communities. 'All we have done', said David, 'is just to give that little bit of encouragement, but most of the work has been done by the Sudanese themselves.' Participation is the key to all David Sharland's work.

David comes from a family with a long line of CMS con-nections. His parents both worked in the Sudan and he grew up with a great interest in Africa. His commitment to Christ deepened from the age of fifteen. From school, he went into horticultural training and then into a business in Devon. His call to serve overseas came through his study of the Bible and the influence of Christian friends. In 1982, he applied to CMS, hoping to go to the Sudan, but was sent to Tanzania where he worked for six difficult but rewarding years in rural development. Then on leave in Britain, he was asked to go to Zaire.

Zaire, a large, beautiful country, is not just forest and pygmies, he says. There are the grasslands where few trees grow and the green rolling hills. He has come to love it deeply, and its people, who live in scattered rural communities, are magnificent. There are three main tribal groups: the Kakwa in the north (Jesse is a Kakwa and so are many of the Sudanese refugees), the Lugbara in the centre and the Alur in the South. But political instability has robbed the people of their happiness. Most people long for a change from the oppressive military regime of President Mobutu. The soldiers, who are not always paid, turn to looting and because they are well-armed, there is little people can do. One night, for example, David found his home surrounded by soldiers firing guns over his roof. Although he was relieved that they did not enter and loot his home, the scene of devastation when they left was unbelievable. Almost every house and shop had been cleared and the people left dazed and powerless. Hyper-inflation is the other problem. Whereas three years ago one million zaires would buy a car, today they will buy about three tomatoes. It is impossible for ordinary people to buy or sell crops: they can only barter.

Most of David's work, which covers an area about the size of Wales, is in the villages around the town of Aru where he set up a rural development centre. A small workshop, office, and all the projects are co-ordinated by Isaac, who left schoolteaching to work more directly for the church and to be the centre's manager. Farmers come to look at examples of animal husbandry, crop planting and rotation, and work with hand-operated machines. There is no electricity in the area or running water. People may come and make use of machines to extract oil from sunflowers, to shell or press oil from peanuts. They cannot afford to buy ready-made cooking oil and the use of hand-made peanut oil offers a real service to the community. Isaac also runs a small shop selling seeds, soya beans, hoes, pangas (bush knives), essential chemicals, and many other commodities.

Quite a large team of workers focus on the centre. One man, who was supplied with tools and trained in carpentry, now makes rabbit hutches, donkey carts, wheelbarrows, bee-hives and furniture. Donkeys were bought from Karamoja for breeding and to be made available to the community for transporting water, crops, and firewood. From a tree nursery, young saplings are supplied to create a supply of firewood and for planting out in areas threatened with soil erosion. The fast-growing leguminous types (such as Leuceana, Acacea or Sesbania) actually improve the soil as they grow. From other areas, requests have come for help and tools for felling trees and cutting timber. David encourages them to replant hardwoods, like teak and mahogany, to provide for their children and grandchildren.

David and Jesse believe that care of the environment is a Christian responsibility to be encouraged in rural Africa. God has given many resources even in Africa, but increased population and intensive farming have led to their deterioration. David and Jesse often include Bible study in training sessions to encourage responsible stewardship. 'It is more natural there', says David 'to accept Bible teaching on the care of God's earth when one digs it day by day, relying on the mercy of the sun, wind and rain, than it is for those of us who shop at Tesco's!'

A team of animators, or motivators, have been selected by their own communities to work among them. David Sharland has been responsible for their training and works with them. They bring requests from the local community for developments they would like to see and if David has ideas they can take them back for discussion by the community. Too often in the past, brilliant ideas for development have been put into action by energetic development workers, only to find that when they leave, the projects are neglected because the people have not been encouraged to be part of the process of thinking them through. If a project is to be of lasting benefit, it must be conceived deep within the community. Once the idea or need is expressed, David can make suggestions or observations. This is where the motivators play a significant role, as mediators or 'bridges' between the village communities and David and Jesse. They each have their own land and are encouraged to develop farms which in turn can become centres to which other farmers come to learn.

In one village David was asked to build a bridge. This was not really the work of a horticulturist, but David learnt how it was done and helped the people to build it. Again, local participation was important. David provided the expertise and some of the materials, including some metal weld mesh which had to be imported from Uganda, but all the hard work was done by the people. And although it began as an Anglican initiative, the whole community was involved: Catholic, Protestant and non-Christian. 'It was exhausting work', says David, 'but how rewarding to see co-operation instead of rivalry.'

In other areas, he has been asked to help protect springs, in order to provide clean water. In some areas, he has encouraged fish-farming co-operatives. Soldiers can come and take their goats, chickens, or even crops, but fish are difficult to steal! This really caught the people's imagination and there was no shortage of labour. About fifteen tons of soil have to be moved for each pond, all by hand. About fifty ponds (each 15m x 10m x 1m deep) have been created, with David showing them how to dig and maintain them and providing the initial stock of fish (Nile Tilapia).

Another non-horticultural challenge came from a parish: to help them tile the roof of a new church they were building! Using local clay, David provided moulds and a machine that looks like a mangle to press the clay into an even thickness. Then the tiles were dried and fired. This technique will in time help people in that area to construct more permanent homes from local materials.

Much of David's and Jesse's time is taken up with practical tasks such as any humanitarian aid worker might do. 'If it were not for my faith in Christ', says David, 'all that would be worth little. But Jesus challenges us to live with practical, servant love that reaches to the poorest, weakest, and most needy, in his name.' Everyday at the centre the staff begin together with a Bible study and prayer, seeking God's guidance and protection. Each month, they put aside a day for prayerful planning of the next month. As problems arise, they will often turn to prayer. Sometimes, they plan a visit to a village to include a Sunday, to share in the worship of the local congregation and encourage church leaders. David enjoys preaching and has learnt to keep a 'flexible' sermon in his Bible to enable him to respond to last-minute invitations to preach. Sleeping a few nights in each village gives an opportunity to chat around the fire and build deeper relationships. 'Many deep fears and doubts are drawn out in the warm atmosphere of the night!' They have a twelve-volt slide projector which runs off their motor bike battery and sometimes show a series of slides featuring the life, death, and resurrection of Christ. They found this a very popular and powerful gospel medium and made translations of the tape for the different language areas.

David has faced spiritual darkness both in communities where fear of the satanic holds people in a very powerful grip and in the opposition of those who resent his philosophy of empowering the poor. As the only white person for miles, he has known loneliness, but also 'incredible companionship', the spiritual and material fellowship of local people. He has faced physical danger from armed bandits on hazardous roads and sickness, but in all these experiences, he has been 'carried through' by an awareness of God's loving presence which comes from disciplined personal prayer and the prayers of others.

Challenges are endless and David's hope is that the collective vision of church and community, fired with imagination and energy, is helping to build God's Kingdom, improving the quality of life for all and bringing benefit to generations yet unborn.

Partnership means equality

MOUSSA and MARGARET CONTEH –
Sierra Leone to Britain

Moussa Conteh had a Muslim upbringing and started to read the Qur'an at the same time as he started school. Later he trained as a primary school teacher at what was then known as Union College, an ecumenical teacher training college, in Bunumbu in eastern Sierra Leone. That was his first contact with a Christian institution. At first it was an obligation to attend morning prayers and worship on Sunday, but the new faith came to have meaning for him and he became the first Christian in his family, and happily there is no conflict or tension with them over his religious commitment. His village has no church. The only Christian presence there was the Catholic primary school and even that was destroyed recently by rebels who invaded from Liberia.

After graduating from Njala University College (University of Sierra Leone) in 1975, Moussa Conteh taught in various secondary schools in Sierra Leone, the last being a Catholic secondary school at Bo in Southern Province. But, feeling that he wanted to 'change direction', he took advantage of an opportunity to discuss his interest in rural development with Bob Dixon, a missionary at Tikonko Agricultural Extension Centre. Bob suggested that he joined the staff there and put him in charge of the extension programme. After a year's practical experience, he came to Reading University in 1981 and did a master's degree in rural social development. On his return in 1982, he took over full responsibility for the Tikonko Agricultural Extension Centre as co-ordinator.

Tikonko Agricultural Extension Centre opened in 1968 in response to the concern of a circuit of the Methodist

Church in Sierra Leone about the shortage of food in the rainy season. A review of its work in consultation with representatives from the village in 1979 led to an integrated approach to development work in the villages, with primary health care and nutrition education, constructing wells, latrines, multi-purpose drying floors and so on.

Margaret Saidu, a nurse of outstanding quality and ability, who had trained at the Nixon Memorial Hospital at Segbwema and qualified as a State Enrolled Community Health Nurse, joined the team at Tikonko to start the primary health care programme. She set up and ran village clinics in Tikonko Chiefdom, training traditional birth attendants and holding classes in health and baby care. She was given study leave to obtain a certificate in tropical community medicine and health at Fourah Bay College, University of Sierra Leone. In 1988, with the support of Moussa, to whom she became betrothed, she left to work for a British Medical Research Council project on river blindness in villages in the Bo district, holding clinics and performing surgical operations to remove nodules from patients infected with river parasites.

The major part of Moussa's responsibility was rice production, working with farmers to increase yields, introducing new varieties of rice seed and improving agricultural methods. A small workshop designed and produced small tools, a vegetable garden demonstrated ways of producing onions, tomatoes, and aubergines, and a bee-keeping project helped to improve the quality of honey. Moussa introduced oxen for ploughing and rabbits to supplement protein. Chickens were imported from Spain to prevent inbreeding and improve on unit quality. He had plans for making it a national bee-keeping centre so that honey need not be imported. The success of the programme brought Moussa Conteh and his staff a great sense of fulfilment and many local farmers looked to them for help and encouragement. There was much more to be done at Tikonko.

Then one day, while he was discussing his work with a visitor from Christian Aid which helped to fund the Centre, the visitor told him of an appointment advertised for the post of Christian Aid Area Secretary for the Chilterns. 'Why not apply and come and work with us,' the visitor suggested. This was a new challenge, to shift the scene of his partnership with Christian Aid.

Moussa and Margaret Conteh are now based in Milton Keynes. Moussa services Christian Aid support groups in the area, visiting local committees, preaching and speaking in churches that support Christian Aid, looking for new contacts, relating to the work of other NGOs like Oxfam and CAFOD and receiving overseas visitors to share in his meetings. To keep up-to-date with new developments, every three years he is given an opportunity to visit a country funded by Christian Aid, to listen to stories of achievement and experience and take photographs to use in Christian Aid's promotional work in Britain. He visited South Africa and Mozambique in 1990 and Brazil in 1993, bringing firsthand experience of Christian Aid's work to his workshops and other area meetings. In particular, he has emphasized the need to support groups like the South Africa Council of Churches, Diakonia and legal aid resource centres who are working for a more peaceful and just South Africa.

Much of Moussa's work is related to fund-raising, especially in Christian Aid Week. He tries to open people's minds so that they give meaningfully, in proportion to their means. The contrasts of lifestyle between Britain and Sierra Leone are stark: we have not really faced up to what it means to *share* resources, he says.

There is an educational side to his work—to raise awareness of the issues, to help launch major campaigns and appeals, and to encourage people to take action and write letters to MPs over matters like the international debt crisis, overseas aid, and injustices of world trade. Disappointingly though, not many go 'beyond giving', he says. He encourages people not only to ask questions—Why give aid to these countries? What is the background?—but to be critical. The UN, for example, goes into Somalia with relief from time to time, but the problems are ongoing and need continual support such as Christian Aid and other NGOs offer. Ideals like 'self-reliance' are difficult to implement. World structures are weighted against developing countries. If we face the problems realistically, we can see that there will never come a time when they will have sufficient means unless we translate our vision of 'One World' into more radical ways of sharing—siphoning resources from affluent countries to help the poor.

Our attitudes have to change, Moussa says, and we need to become more informed about what is really happening in other parts of the world—not just what the media tell us. He leads workshops on the media to counteract the negative images and stereotyping they perpetuate and which find expression in xenophobia. So often the media focus on one small area of a country and give the impression that the whole country is affected by the disturbance. 'How would British people feel', he asks, 'if a TV crew came in from Sierra Leone and, with their coverage of one race riot, gave the whole world the impression that this is how British people live?' Commenting on the British media at a conference in Zimbabwe, he said, 'They give excellent reports, but they can never really feel for the people in the situations.'

Moussa Conteh is Mende-speaking. The Mende frequently bring God into their conversation. When someone asks, for example, 'How are you?' the reply is 'Thanks be to God.' There has been so little appreciation of this and the profound values expressed in their tradition and way of life. Instead, Moussa is acutely aware of a 'colonial mentality' which expects other peoples to measure up to British standards. They have even persuaded Africans to believe in them, so that whatever Africans do, they feel inadequate. 'We've got to look back', he says, 'to find out who we are and what we stand for. This does not mean insularity. African peoples can borrow and use ideas from other cultures, but our foundation for life should be African and not judged by those who come from outside. This only entrenches the inferiority felt.' A visit to Tanzania in 1992 impressed Moussa. East Africans have gone further in restoring their people's dignity and culture and consequently have a sense of national identity. President Nyerere's Ujaama Philosophy—African socialism and self-reliance, evidenced in the many cottage industries he visited—appealed to him.

Moussa's decision to come and share in this work was because he felt this was where God wanted him to be and through it he has discovered the encouragement and strength that come from working in partnership with such a large team of people with common aims and beliefs. 'Christian Aid', he says, 'is not just another charity. The ethos of our work is putting into practice the teaching of Christ. Without that foundation and focus, the work would be reduced to mere human effort, devoid of meaning.' Partnership means equality, he says, and this is evident in the way he is used by Christian Aid and other development agencies. Moussa's contribution is highly valued. His views are sought on matters of policy-making and, through regional and national conferences, he is able to share his insights on a wider scale.

He is respected especially for the sharp challenge he brings to thinking about development. In a paper he was invited to write for Christian Aid about development education, Moussa attacked the fundamental premise of so many in the 'North': that for the South to develop, it must become like the North. He pointed out that the North has so often talked of 'taking development to the South' and plans have mostly been made in the North. Even the Brandt Report was written in Europe! Part of the joy of working with Christian Aid is that people at the grassroots are fully involved in initiating and planning projects. He writes: 'Development education should help us to redeem our dignity and value in our own eyes first and that should arm us to challenge and fight and restore what we were first robbed of as a result of colonization. . . development education should put us in the driving seat to our future, a future that is tied up with the rest of the world.'

Moussa's experience in Britain has been fairly positive, but his wife's experience is another story. Margaret left Sierra

Leone in 1989 with Lamina, their first son, to join Moussa. Her first shock was when she applied for a nursing job and was turned down without an interview. Her qualifications, which are higher than the British SEN certificate, were not recognized here. Furthermore, although according to West African tradition they were husband and wife, in the eyes of British law they were only 'engaged' and Margaret was not permitted to work until after their 'marriage' in 1990. So for the first three months, while they arranged the wedding, she was at home, bored and lonely. Because there was only one income, there was no spare cash to send to Sierra Leone to pay for one or two members of their family to join them for the ceremony. Later, when she was expecting Manga, their second child, and wanted her mother to be with her, there were so many difficulties over her visa before she was permitted to enter Britain. Reflecting on the quality of hospitality and warmth of welcome given to strangers in her country, she felt hurt and angry. Many of her expatriate friends have had similar experiences.

Eventually Margaret got a job as Care Assistant at a home for the elderly in Newport Pagnell. Although they accepted her nursing qualifications and experience and promoted her to Grade 2, she is disappointed that her gifts are not fully used. What hurts most are the attitudes of her patients. Sometimes they swear at her and call her a 'black bastard'. Some of them reject her: 'We don't need you here. Take your black hands off me. Why don't you go home?' Some might be excused as suffering from dementia, but they express the attitudes of a lifetime. Margaret comes home very upset but holds on to the job to help them survive as a family. Lamina, whom they have brought up to be bilingual, is now at school. Mostly he enjoys it but sometimes returns home upset by discriminatory comments from other pupils.

She says, 'I never knew words like "racism" and "prejudice" until I came to this country. The England I used to imagine at home is not the real England I have seen. It was naive of me to think that all white people are very rich and have no problems. I thought all was well with them. I was shocked when I learned there is poverty here as well, though quite different from our own poverty back home. I could hardly believe that people are forced to sleep on the streets in this country.' She adds, 'As I have reflected on the tremendous cultural wealth we have back at home, I have come to appreciate and value my country and people.'

Out of these experiences, a new vision has emerged for Moussa and Margaret: to promote a more positive appreciation of what it means to be African. Moussa believes that mission and development agencies can make a great contribution here. 'Development', he says, 'is not just about sinking wells and providing food, but restoring the culture of my people, enabling them to believe in themselves, increasing their confidence.' This means that literacy and education must be given a higher profile. Interest in writing starts in childhood and needs to be more of a priority in primary schools. This will be difficult. While schools in Britain agonize over the number of computers they can afford to provide, schools in Sierra Leone have no chalk, pens, or pencils.

Traditional African stories need to be researched, documented and published, not only in Africa but here as well. Moussa is inviting writers from Africa to publish their work here and is pointing those who attend his workshops to the wealth of African literature, including children's stories, already available. British Christians should be asking their librarians to stock them.

In a few years, when he returns to Sierra Leone, Moussa plans to work towards making this vision a reality—to encourage cultural research, collect stories and bring together an editorial team to publish them and translate some into English. He wants to promote literacy programmes, to encourage people to write their feelings and experiences. And he has bought a piece of land where he plans to set up a development centre to help his people to understand the issues and empower them so that they can become 'architects of their own future'.

Sharing suffering and death

MONICA JONES –
Britain to Ethiopia and Jordan

'Every day is precious, to be used to the full,' says Sister Monica, who spends most of her time caring for patients dying of terminal disease in a British hospital. 'They are also deprived,' she says, 'and so are their loved ones who watch them die.' Her role there is purely pastoral, 'to awaken them to the life that is within them, so that they can die in peace.'

Sister Monica was educated in a school of the Cross and Passion Order in Bolton. Then, she says with a twinkle of amusement, through the encouragement of her boyfriend's form master, a Salesian priest, she joined the Franciscan Missionaries of the Divine Motherhood and became involved in medical work. When, three years later, the Order was given a plot of land by the government of Zimbabwe to build a new hospital at Bulawayo, she was asked if she would like to go. This was in 1953, before independence. She was very happy there and loved the people. Between 1974 and 1977 she worked in the medical laboratory attached to the mother and child health care clinics in Jordan. The patients were mostly Palestinian refugees.

In 1985, she was asked to go to Ethiopia, in one of its worst famines, to serve with the Mother Teresa Sisters at Dira Dawa. There for two months she worked at feeding centres with another Sister, caring each day for at least four hundred mothers and babies. They provided them with rice, milk, and protein biscuits, looked after their eyes and teeth and helped with a variety of other problems. The most harrowing moment of each day was in the early morning as she made her rounds to find which babies, and sometimes which mothers, had died. And there were happier moments when others recovered and went home. The media often do Ethiopians an injustice when they only portray them reduced to basic necessities. Sister Monica became aware of the outstanding dignity, tenacity, pride, and culture which transcended moments of bitter anguish.

Next she was sent to live in the town to help the local priests with feeding centres in the mountains. This was an exhausting routine: a daily drive of two and a half hours, treating up to three hundred people with scabies and other symptoms of malnutrition and then, after an orange and a cup of coffee, driving the long journey home again.

Just seven kilometres from Dira Dawa, in a small community called 'Village of Hope', they re-established a clinic and a laboratory to assist diagnosis. Sister Monica trained an Ethiopian girl to identify infections and then to take over complete responsibility. It continues to the present day. Handing over to local people was one of the most satisfying parts of her work. Catholic Relief Services, with whom she worked here, had four to five thousand families on its register in each of seven centres. She was proud to identify herself with their programme, but was angry at the ineffective help offered by the government.

Travelling in the mountains one day, an Ethiopian priest turned and asked her what was wrong. 'I'm frustrated with your government,' she replied. 'When the famine started there was plenty of grain, but by the time they gave permission for it to be used, four thousand people had died in these mountains.'

And she was angry with the West. 'As we went to church at 6.15 a.m.', she said, 'we could see lorries full of fresh fruit from the mountains being brought down to the station for export—Ethiopian mangoes to be sold in London—to pay western nations for supplying armaments for the war in Eritrea. Then in the evening, you would see the lorries of aid agencies arrive to distribute sacks of grain to starving people. When you see it with your own eyes, you get angry! Why does the West allow this to happen?'

In 1986, Sister Monica returned to Jordan, where health services, hospitals, and the general quality of life had

improved beyond recognition, but many of the Palestinian
refugees were still there. Some had been in the camp since
1948. Their living conditions were very hard. Again, she
looked after antenatal and mother and child clinics and
trained a local Arab girl with two years' college training to
take over the laboratory. The underlying need in this male-
dominated society was to give these women some sense of
self-worth and involve them in setting up their own projects.
Through a family who came in with a harelipped baby, the
Sisters discovered a Bangladeshi camp just four kilometres
from their clinic. They had no electricity, no sewage disposal,
and only one tap between about fifty families. The Sisters
encouraged them to form their own committee and plan
what to do. One of the Sisters contacted the authorities to
ask for help and the men did the manual work. They now
have clean water, electricity, a school, and a clinic and their
children are learning Arabic. The Sisters helped them to
understand their rights, and trained them so that they could
apply for passports and work permits. The Sisters have tried
and tried to get them recognition in Jordan. It is a case of
going from one government office to another with the
hope that something will be done in the end.

Sister Monica was also involved with the 'Needy Child'
programme. Children were eager to learn, though prospects
of employment were bleak. In another area, they adopted
sixty tuberculosis families. Another project, 'Adopt a
Village', gathered together village elders to discover the
needs of their community and involved them in setting up
plans for its development.

After the Gulf War, as soon as refugees started pouring in,
the Sisters had to divide their time between this project and
the borders where they worked with a team of about forty
workers for NGOs and others at a large transit camp.
Hundreds of refugees were brought each day in large buses
and unloaded there in the middle of the desert, crowding
together in tents, all waiting for planes to take them to
India, the Philippines, the Sudan. . . One million people
were making their way to safety. Jordan is a poor country,

though the affluent residents of Amman 'are hardly aware of the immense needs of thousands of people on the border', she said.

Just recently, since her return to the UK, Sister Monica has spent some time learning from the experience of a hospital in London which cares for many who are dying of AIDS. Here a team of counsellors and two full-time chaplains help people suffering from this devastating disease to find peace before they die. 'You don't have to go out of Britain', she says, 'to go to the poor and marginalized.' She went on to speak of the sense of being abandoned and the prejudice by which such people are surrounded. Her time at this hospital she describes as a profound experience; 'the whole ethos is so Christian.'

Sometimes, convents have been accused of closing out the world, but Sister Monica's experience with the Franciscans has made her more aware of humanity and deepened her understanding of the suffering of ordinary families. Franciscan missionaries aim to be found with those who are most deprived—on 'the cutting edge'—where few will go. Yet none of the suffering she has witnessed has diminished her faith in a God of love. 'God is there in the middle of all this,' she says. 'That is what missionary work is.' Seeing the suffering has helped her to believe more and to understand the meaning of prayer. She has come to a deeper relationship with God. 'In the face of all really deep human suffering', she adds, 'God is the only one who can help.'

Towards 'Health for all by the year 2000'

ADRIAN and SYLVIA HOPKINS – Britain to Zaire

The first eye operation Adrian Hopkins performed at Pimu Hospital in Zaire was on the mother of his chief theatre nurse. He had tried to discourage her, but when her son knew that the surgeon had observed one eye operation during his vacation at Karawa, he reminded him that they had the instruments. So in trepidation and with a large audience, he removed his first cataract! It took a long time and he did not have the help of the magnification that came later but, beginning with totally blind patients— knowing that he couldn't make their sight any worse—he was able to open a weekly eye clinic and gradually increase the service to three times per week with an assistant who sees patients daily.

Until that first operation, the nearest hospital with an eye clinic was three hundred miles away and Adrian was concerned that most of those who needed help were suffering from simple cataracts—otherwise they were healthy people. The work of the clinic at Pimu has been developed in partnership with the Christoffel Blindenmission in Germany who provided equipment. Bosele, his assistant, has also learnt basic surgery for cataract and glaucoma and together they have been able to respond to invitations for help within the Pimu health zone and beyond. Surgery is now performed in sixteen different centres. A workshop has been set up to make spectacles and modify second-hand ones. They produce about six hundred pairs per year; more could be produced if materials were available. Ophthalmic work takes up about a third of Adrian's time.

It was at the end of his first year at university that Adrian felt challenged to offer for overseas service, as he listened to a missionary from Bangladesh at a Baptist Missionary Society (BMS) summer school. At the same time he had begun to reflect on what it meant to be a fully committed Christian. He had noticed how students flocked to hear a good preacher and when that preacher left, they ceased to attend. In Christian Union they were keen to discuss Christian issues but reluctant to give time to decorate slum properties for the elderly in the town centre. Commitment, he believed, involved action, offering all our gifts for the work of the Kingdom and continuing even in difficulties.

During his time at university, a three months' 'elective' in Kimpese, Zaire, was an unforgettable experience. He saw poverty and overworked doctors, and realized that his future role lay in helping to meet those needs. In the next six years he completed his qualifications, married, and became the father of twin sons, Simon and John. Sylvia, his wife, who had qualified as a primary teacher, had felt called to serve overseas, possibly in Bangladesh. Her first teaching post in Bradford was in a reception centre for Asian children. In vacations, they attended various BMS summer schools and were deeply influenced by what they learnt from missionaries serving in Africa and Asia. Their offer to work anywhere was accepted by the Baptist Missionary Society and they were appointed to medical work in Zaire. They arrived in Kinshasa on 1 July 1975.

After two months' orientation in Kimpese and Kinshasa, they set off for Pimu, a remote rural community with a widely scattered population, just across the equator. Unfortunately, Adrian walked straight into a hospital dispute about the use of missionary personnel. Angry crowds gathered outside the house of the other doctor, yelling at the missionaries to return home, a situation for which they were unprepared! It was provoked by a competent, caring, but power-seeking, male nurse.

Generally speaking, in the 1970s there were not enough national doctors to go around and those who had qualified tended to opt for better equipped urban hospitals. So Pimu Hospital had no Zairian senior staff and missionaries were brought in to carry responsibility. Some local staff were resentful. Missionaries appeared rich to them, despite the sacrifice of two good appointments that Adrian had turned down in Britain to come to Zaire! And there were cultural differences regarding the cause of disease and a traditional sense of fatalism. Forward planning and preparing budgets, they said, were western ideas. Their understanding of nursing care was different: Zairian nurses only expected to carry out simple diagnosis and treatment, leaving the patient's family to tend him or her. It was not acceptable for a member of another tribe to perform these tasks. It was a delicate situation and when it was finally resolved after many agonizing months, Adrian had the difficult task of building relationships and trying to maintain standards in a declining economy. All this requires patience and sensitivity.

Adrian and Sylvia's third son, Mark, was born in their second year. After their first furlough they were posted to Kimpese Hospital, and later to Yakusu, before returning to Pimu to help in a staff crisis. Back in Pimu, they were happy to participate in some exciting changes in the role of the hospital.

At this time, it was commonly recognized that despite the work of hospitals and medical staff in developing countries, the communities around them remained trapped in a spiral of poverty, malnutrition, and illness. Diseases like tuberculosis and measles continued their hold in areas where there was poor sanitation, impure water, a lack of nutritious foods, and often overcrowding. By 1970 the World Health Organisation (WHO) had launched its 'health for all by the year 2000' campaign. In the developing world, traditional hospital-based care was very expensive, over-specialized and too dependent on imported drugs. Agencies like Unicef, who saw need for change, began to establish village health services in addition to relief aid. In 1978 WHO and Unicef at a conference at Alma Ata (in the former USSR) agreed to develop the principle of 'primary health care' and declared that health, which is physical, mental and social well-being, is 'a fundamental human right'.

These changes were becoming evident in Pimu. During the 1960s surveys had been carried out to assess the health of the population, especially of children, and this led to establishing village clinics and two village dispensaries. A leprosy control programme began in the 1970s, introducing the new multi-drug therapy which enables some patients to be discharged within six months instead of after five years or more and others after two years rather than lifelong treatment. The number of leprosy patients has reduced from three hundred and twenty in 1980 to sixty in 1990. All patients are out-patients unless there are complications. In 1974 a mobile team started visiting twenty different centres for prenatal and under-five child care. This quickly led to the reduction of measles and tuberculosis. Polio was eradicated.

In the 1980s the government of Zaire introduced its policy of primary health care and divided the country into 'health zones', each one centring on an existing hospital, including Pimu. The Pimu zone being the third largest in the country, it was a great challenge to plan developments for such a vast area of small, scattered communities. They had already built more dispensaries and, in consultation with other state and private dispensaries, these changed into 'health centres'. A health centre is run by a nurse and is responsible for all the curative care, preventive medicine, and health promotion in a clearly defined area. Serious cases are referred to the hospital. Almost double the number of vaccinations are given for half the outlay. Village health workers, or 'paramedics', help the nursing staff. They are usually chosen by the villagers from within their own community and are a vital link with the health centre. Their work includes the under-fives clinic, inoculations, family planning, and adult education training sessions in hygiene and nutrition.

Initially, Sylvia's role was confined to looking after and teaching their three children, helping Adrian with letters, and later on with bookkeeping. When the children were old enough to join the American mission boarding school, she worked as hospital treasurer for several years until she could begin handing over to a trained national. Since then she has been involved in a variety of ways, helping in the pharmacy, teaching other missionary children and latterly teaching non-medical subjects in the nurses' school. Adrian taught her basic eye examination and refraction of spectacles and they usually travel together for eye clinics and surgery.

In 1985, a new airstrip became Pimu's greatest asset, though there was considerable debate as to whether it would really warrant the expense and benefit the community. It took four years to clear an area of forest and level the ground, all done by the community, including relatives of hospital patients. The supply of medicines and drugs via Kinshasa had been slow and expensive, taking anything up to six months. Now they arrive in a day.

In 1985, Adrian was invited to co-operate in writing a training manual on health-zone administration for chief medical officers and zone administrators. This was a team effort, deciding together on the content, and then dividing into subgroups with specific writing tasks which were then drawn together by a small editorial group in consultation with them. Pilot projects were set up to test new ideas and modifications made as necessary. It was an interesting and challenging process, one which opened up opportunities to discuss health issues with colleagues and deepened their sense of community.

Pimu Hospital, which had been built of mud bricks on a concrete foundation from 1932 to 1934, had been difficult to maintain. Paint did not adhere. Insects burrowed into it. Patient trolleys chipped off pieces of walls and it was difficult to keep clean. After part of a ward collapsed, rebuilding commenced in 1988, and in 1990 the official opening celebrated a building of which the staff was justifiably proud. Finally a new church, which Adrian's parents helped to build and which was even more impressive than the hospital, opened in 1991, symbolizing to the community the hospital's role: to bring healing and wholeness in the name of Jesus.

But because of economic chaos in Zaire, it is no longer possible for the hospital to offer free treatment without insisting on a fee. Three quarters of a million dollars was raised for building the hospital, but few are prepared to give to cover running costs. The funding that comes from BMS, the Leprosy Mission, the Christoffel Blindenmission and from the US is not sufficient and the surrounding population lives at subsistence level. Reduction of staff has cut costs but put pressure on those who are left, and sometimes patients do not get the help they need. The very people for whom mission hospitals were established are deprived of treatment and quality care. 'How then', asks Adrian Hopkins, 'do you communicate this to a patient and then tell him or her that you are there to show them the love of God?' This dilemma affects most mission hospitals worldwide.

Zaire's political and economic problems having escalated, Adrian and Sylvia have had to leave Pimu and now work in the Central African Republic with the Christoffel Blindenmission. There Adrian is involved in a new project, working with the government to set up a national plan for the control of river blindness. They are hoping to treat 400,000 people in their first year. As the programme gets underway, the eye clinic set up in Bossangoa—a larger town and focus of the river blindness problem—will become a teaching centre, enabling both preventive and curative work.

Adrian's overall aim has been to combine Christian witness with the highest professional standards. He has played a supportive role in the hospital Christian Fellowship, a group who seek to share their Christian experience with one another and with the patients. When invited to do so, he includes preaching on Sunday as part of his visit to other villages for eye clinics. In one village, for example, the team heard afterwards that everyone on whom they operated had committed or recommitted themselves to Christ.

Looking back over their years of service, Adrian and Sylvia recognize many ways in which their faith has grown and their understanding of life has been enriched by those among whom they have lived and worked. Adrian tells of one Zairian pastor who has been 'brother and counsellor, a closer spiritual colleague than I would ever have experienced in England—a Zairian who is ready to encourage and correct as necessary, who has perhaps come closer to understanding my feelings than anyone else apart from Sylvia.' He adds, 'The experience and job satisfaction far outweigh any lack of financial and career advancement. The challenge comes on returning home to a rich materialistic world—which I enjoy— but which is so in contrast to much of the rest of the world.'

Encouraging the voiceless

STEPHEN and MUKTI BARTON — Britain to Bangladesh

Stephen Barton first heard about India from his father who had served in the Indian navy, but at thirteen his interest was deepened when a local priest introduced him to the poetry of Tagore. In 1970, he hitchhiked to North India and spent six weeks absorbing the ethos and learning from the ways and culture of the people. After completing his degree at Cambridge he travelled to India again, this time teaching as a CMS volunteer in a school in Bihar. He was the only expatriate on the staff. It was there that he met and married Mukti.

They returned to Britain where, after two years' theological training, Stephen became assistant curate of a church in Bradford. Both he and Mukti felt very much at home in

Bradford's multiracial community and Stephen immersed himself in the study of other faiths.

After three years, he began enquiring about the possibility of further work in India. USPG offered him an appointment but Stephen and Mukti were not granted a visa. The Indian government restricts the entry of foreigners to work for the church, as in other types of employment. This disappointment coincided with a letter to USPG from Bishop Mondal of Bangladesh, asking for an assistant priest to care for the English-speaking congregation of St Thomas's Church in Dhaka. So in November 1981 Stephen, Mukti and their two children—Richard who was four and Matthew almost two years old—set off in a slightly different direction from the one they anticipated.

Stephen's work in this city parish was very similar to what it might have been in an urban situation in Britain. After the first year, Stephen had pastoral care of the Bengali congregation as well. This was daunting: it looked like a backward step for St Thomas's. They had had a Bengali minister for the last three years and now they were to have another foreigner! Stephen was aware of how well the Bengali priests knew their people and how hard it would be to communicate effectively in Bengali, despite Mukti's encouragement. But the Church of Bangladesh had so few priests and a city church could cope with an expatriate more easily than a rural congregation. It was a new challenge and would be good for them as a family, so they accepted. His congregation comprised both the relatively affluent and the poor: diplomats and representatives of various aid agencies worshipped with the majority who struggled to survive on very basic wages. It wasn't easy to hold the two together. It was a new challenge to encourage initiatives for the development of the parish to come from members themselves.

Bangladeshi people have a strong sense of community and, from the beginning, Stephen had an affinity with them, especially through Mukti, a Bengali herself. They called him 'Brother' and 'Father', expressing family solidarity with him rather than just ecclesiastical respect. With great sensitivity, he sought to identify himself with their culture, their life, and their needs. Both Stephen and Mukti worked closely with and were deeply influenced by the Taizé Brothers— their commitment to contemplative prayer and human reconciliation, their solidarity with victims of society.

He began to hold weekly courses in basic theology, encouraging his church members to study at home and meet for seminars. Then from 1988 he was invited to help John Webber, another USPG missionary, who was setting up a five- to six-year programme to enable lay people to study theology in their spare time and to prepare for the B Th degree of Serampore (in West Bengal). This involved preparing materials for them to work on at home, holding seminars in the towns and villages where they lived and training indigenous staff to take over the responsibility. Written in Bengali, it was the first Bengali degree course to be taught in Bangladesh. There was an immense thirst to be satisfied among those who registered. Some were full-time church workers—teachers, catechists or wardens of church institutions. Others had ordinary jobs in the community but wanted a more sound understanding of their faith, to be better equipped to serve. Seventy-five out of a membership of 12,000 is a significant proportion of the church to be making a serious study of theology. Some may eventually be ordained, including perhaps the first woman priest in the Church of Bangladesh.

By 1988, having nurtured her children and settled them into school, Mukti began to take up the challenge of women's issues. Bangladeshi women can be divorced on very trivial charges and, as divorcees, are shunned by society. Many are alone and destitute. Even in the family, women are malnourished because they serve themselves last and eat the least. In most cases, women bear the burden of poverty. Often, as a priest's wife, she had listened to their stories and shared their pain.

At first, Mukti was invited by the YWCA and the Christian Council of Churches to talk about mixed marriage and other women's issues and sometimes attended conferences

on them. Then a Methodist woman minister from the US
encouraged her to begin reading feminist theology. Reluctant at first, she became fascinated and soon began to relate
it to everyday life in Bangladesh. She began to 'pray with an
open mind', seeking direction. Stephen had brought home a
theological magazine reflecting on the struggle of women in
Asia. As she read it, Mukti knew instinctively that this was
her calling, to enable women to begin their search for justice.
She continued to read and to attend conferences and courses,
both in Asia and on furlough in Britain. She became convinced that feminist theology made sense of the gospel, not
only for women but for the whole world.

In Bangladesh, feminism was 'taboo'. The few who shared
her vision were frightened to do anything about it and there
was no money. Mukti secured funding from Church World
Services (of the US). One room of their family flat became
known as the Women's Leadership Training Centre.
Mukti, the only full-time worker, covered all the tasks of
programme co-ordinator, accountant, and typist but was
supported by a committee of ten. Their aims were to give
moral and spiritual support to Christian women as they
developed their own theological understanding and sense
of solidarity. They had first of all to build up trust. Women's
loyalty to their husbands and families makes them too often
reluctant to come and open up. But in workshops, what the
women couldn't articulate from their own painful experiences, they could act out. Participation was spontaneous.
Through role play they looked at women in the Bible,
especially in the Gospels, and heard Jesus speaking to them.

Able to see more objectively how women were treated in
the home, they realized that patriarchy had been sanctioned
by the church which made women promise 'to obey'. They
invited pastors and priests to look at these marriage vows
and change them. They encouraged women to challenge
inhuman customs in their villages. Many inhumanities
were brought out into the open. Some women had been
ostracized by the Christian community on account of their
marriage to Muslims. 'It was like removing a cork from a

bottle,' said Mukti. One woman, for example, who was married to a drunkard, had to resort to prostitution to pay for his alcohol. Eventually she ran away with another man and bore him a child, but when he threw her out, she was forced to return to her husband. According to the custom of his village, such a woman should be hung on a tree and beaten. Though inhuman and unjust, the male-dominated church was happy to leave local customs alone. Being encouraged by Mukti, local church women felt moved to seek the support of a human rights organization to save the victimized woman. Another issue is the payment of dowry. Paid by the bride's family to the bridegroom, this is open to exploitation. 'Culture', says Mukti, 'is misused for male interest, but today voiceless women are finding a voice.'

When Stephen and Mukti went to Bangladesh, it was on a three-year contract. Little did they realise they would stay for eleven years. They returned to Britain in 1992 and have settled in Southampton. Stephen's work there is a development of what he was doing in Bangladesh, working with people of other faiths, encouraging dialogue and building relationships.

Mukti's work has not ended either. As well as getting involved in Christian–Muslim perspectives on women's rights here, she has begun research for a postgraduate degree on the subject: 'Liberating women in Bangladesh'. This will include what is being done to help both Christian and Muslim women and will contribute to understanding the issues that affect Bengali women in Britain.

Now that they have worked in Britain for about a year and distanced themselves a little from their experiences in Bangladesh, they are able to reflect. What difference has it made to themselves as a family? How valuable was their contribution to the Church of Bangladesh? What questions remain?

After beginning their education in their home, Richard and Matthew went to school in Dhaka. Education in another culture may not be straightforward. There was no 'ideal school', but they 'lived fully in Bangladesh'. This was important to them as a family and has given the boys a broader perspective to their education and future in Britain. As a family, despite times of frustration and difficulty, they are aware of how much they have received and learnt. There was a simplicity of attitude, an awareness that life is more than the acquisition of possessions.

Eighty-three per cent of Bangladeshis are Muslim. Nationality and religion are almost synonymous, which makes a Bangladeshi Christian a contradiction in terms. Every Bangladeshi is assumed to be a Muslim. This was sometimes difficult for Mukti to handle (Hindus and Buddhists who lived there shared this problem). Stephen and Mukti discovered not only the significance of their Christian identity in a country where everyone is assumed to be a Muslim, but, despite the multiplicity of Christian sects in Bangladesh, their oneness and fellowship with Christians of other denominations. Ecumenical relationships and relationships with people of other faiths came much easier than in Britain. 'In Bangladesh, you had to tell people why you're a Christian,' said Mukti, 'which means you go deep into your own faith.'

Bangladesh, one of the most densely populated and poorest countries in the world, is often associated with cyclones and suffering. Bangladeshis of all faiths are people of resilience and hope, coping with disaster one day and beginning to sow and rebuild the next. There is immense involvement in development and health-care programmes. Bishop Mondal says of the Church of Bangladesh, 'The Church is there to share the self-giving love of Jesus Christ in full solidarity with the people.' Stephen and Mukti learnt to cope with whatever hit Bangladesh and, on reflection, realize how much their faith has been strengthened by sharing the pain. Christ the victim made sense to them there. Conducting funerals in horrendous circumstances, Stephen witnessed Christians singing with devotion to God in the midst of tremendous anguish. Bengali worship cannot be separated from everyday life but is 'from the heart'. It is rooted in the tradition of centuries of Hindu music and poetry which expresses a great love of God (the songs of Tagore are sung by many Christians). There is no pretence. Pain is not ignored but transformed into joyful worship. Bengali Christians know that God suffers with them.

Such integrity in the face of disaster led Stephen and Mukti to a realization that 'God is within, at the heart of things—not up there.' Returning to Britain, they were surprised to hear the triumphalist note of Christian songs of the 1980s, dominated by the image of an omnipotent God. Faced with divine vulnerability in the anguish of Bangladesh, the image of a 'powerful' God could only be the heresy of those who cling to the former domination of the British Empire, not the gospel.

Receiving the gospel from the poor

JAMES and SUSAN GROTE – Britain to El Salvador

In November 1992, at the annual assembly of the El Salvador Baptist Association, a huge banner hung facing the delegates. On it were two rifles, each distinctively different from the other, symbolizing the two sides of the twelve years' civil war, but their barrels were knotted together. The two lines of barbed wire below had been cut, while growing up between them were green leaves and a stalk opening out, before the rising sun, into a full ear of corn. It was a sign of hope in a country nearing the end of a long saga of negotiations for peace.

James and Susan Grote and their two children, Daniel

and Cameron, went to El Salvador in August 1991 as missionaries with the Baptist Missionary Society. Their interest in El Salvador had grown over ten years of receiving visitors from El Salvador, their involvement in a local solidarity group in Derby, and James' visit to the country as a member of a British delegation in 1988.

They felt a tremendous sense of privilege to arrive at such a significant time in the history of what Jon Sobrino has called 'a crucified people'. The roots of this cruel war span five centuries of exploitation by the 'Conquistadores' and repression of the indigenous culture. The El Salvadoran currency which bears the image of Christopher Columbus is a reminder of the struggle. In 1932 thousands of peasants, led by outlawed trade unions, rebelled against their conditions and 30,000 were killed by the army. For the next fifty years they were ruled by the military, whose answer to persistent demands for a more just distribution of wealth was repression and death squads. In 1980, a coalition of opposition movements, the Farabundo Marti National Liberation Front (FMLN) began to wage guerrilla warfare on the US-backed government and military. Since then over 75,000 people have been killed. The majority of families, especially among the poor, can add names of relatives to the list of those who were harassed, tortured, died, or disappeared.

For the first four months, James and Susan were given time in the capital, San Salvador, to settle their children into school, to learn the language, and get used to being in a country with so many challenges. It was an opportunity to learn from the churches' response to injustice and war, like the Centre for Youth Protection established by the Baptist Association in 1988 to help families trace their missing sons. Young men were taken by force from buses and on the streets, to join one of the battalions with no notification given to their families. James and Susan were introduced, for example, to the work of SAN, the health and literacy programme of the Baptist Association. Susan was taken to visit Rutilio Grande, a community named after a priest who was

murdered by a death squad in 1977. On the way, they passed
three small crosses marking the place where Rutilio Grande
and the two young people who were with him were murdered. The settlement comprised sixty families who had
returned from exile in Honduras. Within six months they
had built houses and a clinic, and were in the process of
sinking a well and building a school. Another visit with
SAN to a group in the west turned out to be a celebration
of the Day of the Child. The pulpit was pushed to one side
and a pair of scales put in its place. The minister weighed
the children and filled in their record chart. Someone else
gave them Vitamin A drops.

In the closing hours of 1991, after twenty months of
negotiations, the Peace Accord between the El Salvador
government and the FMLN was signed in New York at the
United Nations. For the following two days, James and
Susan witnessed a great fiesta in the Cathedral Square of
San Salvador. Banners of the FMLN and all the movements
who had been involved were displayed. At midday an
ecumenical service was held to symbolize the sacrificial
role of the church throughout the years of civil war. It was
Epiphany, a poignant reminder of the light that cannot be
extinguished.

Yet joy was tinged with fear and a sense of the fragility of
peace. Two days later, a priest was arrested on the charge of
being a guerrilla—a charge frequently made against those in
the church who work with the poor. He was released three
days later to await trial. A full agreement to begin a UN-
monitored cease-fire and peace process to end the war was
signed on 16 January 1992 in Mexico City—another occasion
for a fiesta—but what was becoming more important was the
need for groups like the church to plan how to help families
and communities to cope with the aftermath of war. The
Baptist National Assembly had already listed the problems:
violence, fear, delinquency, unemployment, poverty,
inflation. . . A divided country needed the reconciliation
that was at the heart of the gospel.

At the end of January James, Susan and their family

moved to San Miguel, the third largest city of El Salvador. The boys quickly settled into a local Catholic school while James and Susan began to work with a small Baptist church on the edge of the town. James also spends much of his time visiting twenty other Baptist churches in the east of the country, providing pastoral support and help to their ministers and congregations.

The most significant part of their presence has been, and will continue to be for some time, to listen to people's stories and to share the grief and tears of ordinary people whose family life has been irreparably damaged by twelve years of war crimes. Besides a death toll of 75,000, there were 500,000 displaced and one million refugees fled to other parts of Central America, the States and Canada. Some of the trips that James has made have taken him through villages that have been almost completely destroyed. Very often, however, a greater destruction lies beneath the surface, deep in the experiences of people's lives. Visiting and sharing their worship means listening to their stories.

1992 being the bicentenary of the Baptist Missionary Society, James received a number of visitors from Britain and took them to villages like El Mozote to hear the stories too. From 11 to 13 December 1981, the Atlacatl Battalion ringed an area of Northern Morazan, and began killing people in the surrounding villages. Those who fled took refuge in El Mozote. Almost a thousand people were killed there. Only one woman escaped to tell the story. Mothers who were killed in one building could hear the cries of their children being killed in another. The remains of over ninety children's bodies were excavated from the ruins along with their small toys, marbles, and miniature cars. James showed his visitors the church which, like the homes around it, was in ruins, with a cross propped up in front. In the centre of the village, in crude-cut thick metal, was a monument of a man, woman, girl, and boy holding hands, put there on the tenth anniversary of the massacre.

In San Salvador, likewise, the house of Archbishop Romero has become a museum, displaying his personal possessions, calendar, and bloodstained robes from the day he was shot. 'This is what it means to tell the story,' says James. 'Why? To remember. To tell a story, like body and blood, like a man on a cross. It seems quite macabre but, somehow, by telling the story, these things—the robe, the blood, and the story they tell—like the bread and wine, become symbols of hope, life and resurrection.'

A United Nations negotiated cease-fire began on 1 February following the signing of the Peace Accords. The Peace Accords involved changes to the justice and electoral systems, and agrarian reforms to redistribute land held by powerful landowners and the provision of credit for the poor to buy it. They involved economic and social reforms to deal with the country's poverty. The army would be cut by half and its human rights abuses during the war investigated. A new civil police force would be established and the FMLN rebel army demobilized and its arms destroyed. After eleven months of political negotiations, stalemating and pro-crastination, the twelve-year civil war came to an end on 15 December and the FMLN was recognized as a political party. An ecumenical service of thanksgiving was held in one of the parks of San Miguel that day. The gospel for the third Sunday in Advent was Matthew 11.1–15 where Jesus replied to the disciples of John the Baptist that the signs of the Kingdom were in their midst, as broken lives were made whole again and the poor heard the good news. And this was symbolized in the offerings they brought forward—a machete, a cooking pot, a book, pen and paper, a maize plant, and a cross.

James has started to give pastoral support to an art project —a group of seven women designing bookmarks, gift paper, and stationery using traditional El Salvadoran drawings, like the picture of the cross that Christian Aid used on the front cover of the Lenten Study booklet for 1992. This pro-ject was started by a North American missionary and James is helping the women to develop new markets for their work. One design has a woman with outstretched arms, tied to a tree with a rope around her wrists and ankles. In the background are El Salvadoran houses, plants, birds, and animals. Cristela who designed it said, 'It shows what life is like for women in El Salvador. Women here are crucified.' For twelve years, they had borne a great burden of responsibility and mourned the deaths of husbands, sons, and little children.

In less than two years, James and Susan have been stretched in both mind and heart. El Salvador has catapulted them into ecumenical encounters of a nature that would probably have never happened at home. James was invited to share the funeral traditions of a Catholic family into which one of their Baptist friends from the Buenos Aires Mission was married. This was one in a series of nine daily liturgies in the home following the death of Amilcar's mother-in-law. Thirty women had gathered. The focal point was a table on which had been placed a cross, candles, some flowers, and a picture of Jesus. This 'altar' stood between two single beds. The quiet rhythm of the liturgy which lasted for an hour was deeply moving. He was aware of the gulf of prejudice that separated them from other Christians who would have regarded this as 'pagan superstition'. But it remains with him as a powerful symbol of El Salvador and the spiritual strength of its women.

Elena, a newcomer to his congregation, was pouring out her problems to James. Alba, an older woman, whose very literal faith had been nurtured at the Mission, joined them. Leaning back in her chair in the doorway of Elena's house, Alba said, 'It's only really the poor who can understand the gospel; the rich have so many things that take them away from God, the poor have nothing and have to rely on God.' That prompted a discussion on the previous Sunday's Bible study of the parable Jesus told of the great feast where the rich stay away because 'they've got too much to do' and so their places are taken by the poor and handicapped. Here were evangelical Christians making radical connections and a missionary learning from the challenge they made.

James has discovered the truth of Paul's words that God chose the weak to shame the wise (1 Corinthians 1.27–28)—

the poor of El Salvador often understand facets of the gospel that confuse western Christians. He writes, 'The church of the West needs to hear the stories of the poor and listen to their faith and understanding of the gospel. That, it seems to us, is the most important role of missionaries who work amongst the poor—to be channels through which their stories can be heard.' He reminds us of the danger of romanticizing a simplicity which arises out of a daily struggle for basic necessities. Alba said to him on another occasion, 'I'm worried about keeping this house going and making ends meet.' He went on to say that the gospel is about changing their situation, bringing liberty to captives, and freedom to the oppressed (Luke 4.16–19). During the twelve-year war, the poor struggled for that change and to defend human rights. Many were motivated by Christian convictions, including some who entered into the armed conflict by joining the FMLN army. He writes, 'It is not the rich who will change the plight of the poor; the rich have created it in the first place, but it is the poor who will change their own situation.'

The other insight that has come to James is that people do not plan for the future in El Salvador as they do in Britain. In the churches, decisions are made for the oncoming week or two weeks. An anniversary is planned a few weeks before. 'In daily life, where people live from hand to mouth, from one day to the next, the future is tomorrow, or even today's wages, or the next meal.' Unlike those of us whose lives are controlled by full diaries, they are able to respond to unexpected invitations and the needs of those around them. 'There is an immediacy about the gospel and the promise of the Kingdom which is here, now, among us, with a warning not to plan too much or worry about the future.'

A time for obedience

NICHOLAS and CATHERINE DRAYSON –
Britain to Spain

Running a Christian arts festival in Seville was great fun and
what surprised most churchgoers was that it drew together
churches of different denominations, liberals and evangel-
icals, and took place at the heart of drug land. Some drug
addicts and two drug peddlers helped to police it! Nick and
Catherine Drayson, who had a good rapport with Spanish
inner-city drop-outs, did not fit most Christians' stereotype
of 'missionaries'. 'All churches were on the stage together,'
they said. Differences dissolved and the church communi-
cated a united front. Nick and Catherine may not have had
the expertise that others had who took up the idea and
kept it going, but they had the vision to get it started. They
wanted the festival to be a witness to people in one of
the poorest parts of the city and to bring other churches
into this ministry. Willing to be 'fools for Christ', they
saw themselves as 'catalysts'. 'God still wants people to
cross frontiers,' said Nick, 'but in most cases, someone from
outside must go in. Eventually local people will take up the
idea and continue in a way which relates more effectively
to their culture.'

Nick's Christian commitment owed much to his parents
sending him to camps as a child. At seventeen, he experienced a strong turning-point and a growing conviction that
he was being called to full-time work for God, probably
overseas. At eighteen, he went to Mexico to visit a friend
who worked as an agriculturist for Wycliffe Bible Translators.
He returned home, fired with enthusiasm to work among
South American Indians, though at this stage didn't see
where his study of modern languages fitted in. His years at

university were formative ones in which he sought 'to discern God's will'. When he was twenty, he took a year out to teach in a school in Buenos Aires and study at the university there. It was a time of political turmoil and many Argentine Christians were involved in issues of social justice and human rights. The following year, he heard of a request from the Bishop of North Argentina for a linguist to reduce the Chorote language to writing to enable this small tribe of about 2,000 people to translate their Scriptures. He completed his degree and entered a period of training with the Wycliffe Bible Translators. After a brief period of preparation and feeling very raw, he went to Argentina in 1976 under the auspices of the Anglican Church and through the South American Missionary Society (SAMS). For the next six years he studied the Chorote language and began translating the New Testament while also being trained for the priesthood. After his ordination by an Amerindian bishop, he became pastor of the church at Tartagal and continued with his translation work. He would have stayed longer had it not been for the Falklands War.

On his return to Britain, he met up with and married Catherine Le Tissier, a friend from student days at Oxford University, who had not long returned from working for two years in Swaziland.

Catherine came from a Christian Brethren and mission hall background. But it was the stimulus of lively churches in Oxford, where she trained as an occupational therapist, that kindled her faith and gave her vision. Through many South African friends, she began to form a real commitment to Africa. During her two years in Swaziland, through the International Voluntary Service, she was responsible for medical rehabilitation work in Mbabane Government Hospital: helping people to become independent despite disabilities, improving their physical movement, helping carers to cope, trying to get the department better equipped . . . One of the interesting aspects of occupational therapy in a developing country is that it does not require elaborate equipment but, with imagination and initiative, can make use of local resources. She worked alongside a Swazi who had trained in Liverpool and was prepared to take over the department when she left.

After their marriage, SAMS approached Nick and Catherine with an entirely new suggestion: they needed a linguist in Spain to help set up language training for missionaries going to serve in South America and to respond to an invitation from the Spanish Episcopal Reformed Church for pastoral help. Initially, it sounded like a short-term appointment but extended to nine years. On arrival, Nick was asked by the Spanish bishop to plant a church in an inner city area of Seville. It was an enormous challenge, the toughest he had ever faced, but became a rich experience.

In the first place, they didn't expect to be sent to Spain. Their vision and expectations extended to Africa and South America but South West Europe was hardly 'mission field'! Having brought with them all the 'emotional baggage' of leaving Argentina and Swaziland, their first year was a time of much heart-searching, prayer and spiritual battle, and they wondered if they would survive. Nick, debilitated by a tropical illness he had contracted in Argentina, was thrown into a situation where he had to take the lead. This clashed with his mission philosophy: he had hoped he was there to work under indigenous leadership. The process of orientation to a culture against which, deep down, they rebelled didn't help to cope with the stresses of their first year of married life. Neither did it help Catherine to face the vacuum left by not being able to practise her profession. This was a partnership in which Catherine's leadership potential and flair were as great as her husband's and they were both called to persevere in a situation they would not have chosen. Being only a beginner in learning the language, Catherine was unable to communicate effectively and make friends, while Nick spoke fluently. Suddenly she realized that she had relied too much on what she could do: that God loved her and worked through her even when she was at home looking after Sammy, their first child.

The Spanish Episcopal Church, which had not been

founded by missionaries, is over one hundred years old. It is essentially a historical middle-class Church, proud of its past and the struggle for religious freedom, but not adapting too easily to new challenges. For Nick and Catherine this was a case of persevering without immediate success—so unlike their work with the poor in Argentina and Swaziland. Even when they thought they had got right into the culture, they did not feel accepted. It was a time for obedience—'being where God wants you to be, even if you can't see why,' said Catherine. They began by working with the existing core of church members, helping them to develop in prayer, worship, and evangelism and then involving them in every conceivable form of outreach: films, visiting, house-groups. . . An enormous amount of time went into children's activities, both for church members and their friends and for children off the streets, and this led to much breaking down of barriers. Sometimes they were helped by visiting teams from Britain and other parts of Spain. Nick also led missions in other cities where the Episcopal Church works. Many new contacts were made and some real conversions, though many were reticent about joining a non-Catholic church. At last they began to see leaders beginning to emerge, and were encouraged.

Their main task had been helping church families to move from seeing the church as a tradition to discovering 'a living relevant faith in Christ'. It was often hard to hold together the frustrations of the young and the resistance of older members to new ideas, and to spend time with new people coming in, many of whom were psychotics, drug abusers, alcoholics, single parents, prisoners on parole, and 'foreigners'. The presence of people of other cultures gave their church a cosmopolitan atmosphere though it did not always help in their attempts to develop indigenous leadership. Many times, they found that families of drug abusers were very open to pastoral help. At one point they fostered two girls (and their dog) whose parents were both imprisoned on drugs charges.

As time went on, they recognized that the most effective

means of evangelism was through friendship and noticed that as members grew in confidence, they would involve their friends and families. Through such contacts, Nick and Catherine learnt much from the Spanish emphasis on family relationships, their love of children, the tradition of sitting for a long time over meals, building up commitment to one another, and involving everyone.

In contrast to South American Christians who justifiably are critical of their history—five hundred years of oppression —and live for the future, Nick began to see the positive strengths of the Spanish churches in a historical way. There are lessons here, he believes for the church worldwide—to discover our historical roots and a sense of identity. They learnt to respect what the church had achieved and established in the past, unlike those evangelists who rush in as though no one has been there before! They learnt to appreciate some of the strong tradition of well-structured liturgy in the Spanish church. Coming from an evangelical background, and working with other Protestants, they learnt from the Roman Catholic challenge to social involvement and incarnation theology: 'God isn't saving us from this world. God loves the world.' They learnt to respect God as Creator as well as Saviour and to realise that, biblically, ecological concerns are as much mission issues as church growth.

An interesting part of Nick's ministry was the development of ecumenical relationships, partly through the Christian arts festival and partly through the Roman Catholic married priests' fellowship. The latter, who were seeking to put pressure on the Vatican to allow them back into the priesthood, turned to Nick and Catherine for help and fellowship. Initially, they invited them to share their experiences as a man and wife in ministry together. After that, they met with them every month and found this a lively source of fellowship and fun.

One Christmas Eve, Nick was asked by the British Consulate to take Communion to a British journalist, on a drugs charge, in Sevilla Dos high security prison. There, cut off from her family, she had found God. Although Nick continued to take Communion to her, he suggested that Catherine should befriend her and this opened up a whole new ministry for Catherine. The journalist, excited about her new-found faith, began caring for her fellow prisoners and invited Catherine to visit them. They included South Americans, Germans, English and others, usually charged for being found bringing illegal drugs into Spain, few of them aware of the seriousness of their crime. As far as their families were concerned, they had no means of communication and had disappeared. They had no access to legal help. Catherine listened to their problems and, at home, phoned relatives or wrote letters for them.

Catherine contacted consulates and other agencies, including 'Sevilla Acoge', an organization offering advice to foreign prisoners. She attended hearings, collected clothes and shoes for them and offered hospitality to many ex-prisoners on their release. When they asked her to do so, she read from the Bible and prayed with them. A small group formed a Bible study fellowship and invited her to lead them. It was here more than in the church where she discovered real fellowship and God's purpose in bringing her to Spain. The British Consulate was glad for her to be involved and enabled her to change the wording on her work permit from 'missionary' to 'representative of the British Consulate'. Jehovah's Witnesses, Mormons and other *religiosos* were unwelcome.

They returned to Britain in 1993 for the birth of Stefaine and to prepare for the next stage in their journey—to return in January 1994 to Argentina, where Nick will continue helping with the translation of the Chorote Bible. The Gospel of Mark was published in 1992 and the other Gospels and the Acts are complete in rough draft. An Indian pastor whom Nick trained will be working on the texts and Nick, as 'exegete', will ensure clarity and accuracy. As a catalyst again, he will be promoting Indian languages and translations of the Scriptures, so that Indians will have the resources to do their own theology. Another challenge is to identify with the Church's prophetic movement to secure land rights for Indians. They will be stationed in Misión la Paz in the forest, a very isolated area. Catherine will have a baby to look after and Sammy to begin teaching at home. She goes, not as a professional but counting it a privilege to learn from the Indian culture and live like Indian women, carrying water and baking her own bread.

'Mission', said Nick, 'is everything God sends people to do in the whole world.' He went on to point out that those who are called to cross frontiers may be going to do 'church work' as distinct from 'missionary work'. 'Missionaries are ordinary Christians who are sent from their pews to the places where they live and work, to share Christ in word and action.'

Caribbean challenges

RODERICK and WILHELMINA HEWITT – Jamaica to Britain

Roderick Hewitt's early awareness of spiritual values stemmed from the dominant influence of a religious mother –'my mother who fathered me'. His father had migrated to Britain to provide for the family. Brought up in strong Presbyterian traditions, he received an education based on the Knox principles of rigorous intellectual development out of practical experience. His headmaster, Lewis Davidson from the Church of Scotland—a dominant fatherlike person affectionately called 'Pops' by his students—mixed 'faith with works' and gave the school a strong Christian ethos.

Roderick was born in 1953, when Jamaica reached a very

important phase in its struggle for self-rule from Britain. Through the influence of Marcus Garvey, Jamaica's national hero and promoter of political consciousness, he learnt to appreciate what it means to be a Jamaican and not 'an appendix to another body'. Garvey taught Jamaicans to call upon 'God within', the God of black dignity and black awareness. Roderick Hewitt's concept of God began to change 'from a Euro-centric understanding to an agro-centric reality'.

Jamaica achieved independence in 1962. Roderick took pride in identifying with the plurality of Jamaican culture and its motto—'Out of Many, One People.' Here were peoples who had travelled from other parts of the world learning to live together. Martin Luther King's struggle for human rights and justice, and global solidarity with oppressed peoples resonated with all this and was the other major influence in his early life.

As a 'child of the United Church', he valued the ecumenical ethos that resulted from the union of Presbyterian and Congregational churches in 1965 to form the United Church in Jamaica and the Cayman Islands (UCJGCI). Through the youth ministry of the United Church, he grew in understanding both himself and where God wanted him to be. In 1972, as he completed high school education, his mother and sisters migrated to the States but Roderick's cultural and spiritual roots were too strong to follow them and he remained in Jamaica.

Being caught up in the youth movement of the Church, he was encouraged to make a more specific commitment to serve God. It was here that he met Wilhelmina, a teacher and very active youth worker, who became his wife. Youth for Christ challenged him essentially as 'a movement'. His view of Christianity moved beyond the institutional approach: although called to ministry, he didn't want to be 'only a minister'. From 1973 to 1977, as a student at the United Theological College of the West Indies, he began to explore ways of communicating his faith, especially through involvement with the university drama society, where very sensitive social issues, that weren't dealt with in the classroom, were addressed.

After ordination, he began his ministry on the north coast of the island in the bauxite mining, tourist, fishing, and small-scale farming area of Discovery Bay. There he faced congregations with very different expectations, but needing to see their faith in relation to their environment. On one memorable occasion, an elderly lady stopped him in the middle of a sermon. Taking his ideas, she put them in the local context in a way that he had not realized was possible. It was a powerful experience. He learnt that the gospel must be 'incarnated in terms of symbols'. Preaching is a two-way process which begins by 'listening' to those who hear the message.

Aware of a lack of consistency in work with children, he decided to test this new principle 'to listen'. Together with other youth leaders, he began to ask children in one of the congregations why they did not come regularly to Sunday school. And the children began to ask, 'Why do you single us out?' It seemed to them as though the congregation dismissed them to get on with the real and serious task of worship and learning. In response, an all-age educational process was introduced and a hundred years' old tradition was changed. Every age group was involved in learning and each group had to bring something back to the service to share. This was also a powerful learning experience.

Then an invitation came from the United Reformed Church in Britain to the UCJGCI for a minister to come and help in a multiracial area of Birmingham. The change was dramatic. From the blue seas and idyllic scenery of Discovery Bay, Roderick, his wife and their two small children looked out from their new home on to inner city tower blocks. And as they became aware of their 'foreign-ness' to the black community here, as well as to the white, Psalm 137 reverberated with this twentieth century exilic experience—'By the rivers of Babylon we sat down and wept as we remembered Zion. . .'

Their two children, Rochelle and Machel, who were just

ready to start school, integrated well and were the first to become acclimatized (Michael, their third child, came later). Wilhelmina missed the support of the extended family and her teaching job in Jamaica but saw a new role: to help build bridges of understanding.

The first challenge for both of them was when Roderick opened the door to the local Imam and representatives from other faiths in the community, who called to welcome them. From the strong Christian tradition of Jamaica, they had to work out how to relate to another facet of pluralism. Roderick was deeply moved when the Imam invited his colleague Peter Lovett to come and pray for his daughter who was sick. His concept of mission began to grow again. Was it a matter of 'mission to' or 'mission with'?

Another challenge was what he calls 'ordained predictability'. From a Caribbean tradition where the length of sermon was irrelevant, he clashed with the 'nothing more than twenty minutes' syndrome of British congregations! But he found spirituality in unexpected places. He learnt from the quiet reflection of elderly widows in tower block dwellings. They may not have been as articulate about their faith as Jamaican women, but they were dynamic and 'the still small voice' was real and alive in their presence.

1985 was the year of the Handsworth riots and the Hewitts suddenly became aware of marked boundaries—roads that separated one ghetto from another. Black churches were 'black'. White churches might include black members but they were still 'white'. 'In Jamaica, because we were part of the black majority, we have always seen people by name and not by colour,' they said. Roderick began to understand the struggles of black youths harassed by police. He learnt 'to access the system' to get justice. It was good to be 'foreign black' because he could enter both communities as mediator, encouraging them to listen to one another. 'If Christians are to be credible', he says, 'they must cross these barriers. They cannot retreat into a church ghetto, but are called to move out beyond church walls.'

At the end of 1986, Roderick was invited to work with the

Council for World Mission (CWM) who were embarking on a new Education in Mission programme called 'Equipping Local Congregations in Mission'. As they would be moving to London, Wilhelmina, who enjoys working with people, decided to train as a social worker and now works with the child protection unit of social services.

Being a CWM staff member, and having opportunities to travel and consult with other churches, both in Britain and in other parts of the world, has broadened Roderick's horizons still further and given him many opportunities to share the Jamaican Christian perspective with people in Britain and to learn from others. There is so much to learn from the spirituality of Christians of other cultures, learning to sing other people's songs and enter into their emotions. 'Christ has so many faces,' he says. Crossing national frontiers and reading the Scriptures with others has taught him that 'the Lord has more truth to reveal'. In Bangladesh, disturbed in the early morning by the Muslim call to prayer, he gave up the struggle to sleep and got up to pray. 'Why should they pray alone?' he asked. In a Buddhist temple in Taiwan, watching a devout elderly woman lighting a candle and praying with tears, he learnt that prayer is not the exclusive property of Christians: 'There are other ways of encountering God.'

He discovered that exposure to the world Church challenges Christians to eat one another's food, as Peter was challenged in the house of Cornelius (Acts 10). Having come from the Jamaican tradition where the Sunday afternoon meal is the crowning meal of the week, he and the family responded with eagerness to an invitation to Sunday afternoon tea with a British family! He found that the essential ingredient of table fellowship is 'acquiring a taste for different foods, to be able to sit where others sit and eat what they eat—to enter into a faith-learning experience in their context.'

Another learning experience has been through CWM's Training in Mission programme, through which young people from different cultures come together for one year to explore their faith in a variety of ways and to prepare to serve as mission partners in different parts of the world. This is a very powerful experience, being forced to learn what are the fundamentals of faith and what constitutes 'baggage'. Denominationalism and nationalism go out of the window as young people hear Christ speaking to them in a variety of ways, not only as individuals but 'in community'.

From the time he began to think about committing himself to the service of God, Roderick Hewitt has been deeply concerned about the renewal of the church's mission. He believes the ordained ministry needs restructuring so that it is seen as only one important element in mission. 'A church cannot afford to be clergy-centred if it is to break new ground in the world. Ordained ministers are equippers, not monopolisers of the church's mission,' he says pointing to the Latin American Base Christian Communities and the way the Church of South India is enabling local congregations to engage in mission.

Both Roderick and Wilhelmina see these wider experiences as a preparation for their next step—'a reimmersion into the Jamaican context'. Wilhelmina, with her qualification in social work, will be able to make a real contribution to Jamaican society where social services are still in their infancy. And Roderick plans to enable Jamaican Churches to share their many strengths and insights with the world Church.

South to South mission

HANNOCH and MARJORIE MARMA DUKE – South India to Jamaica

'Here am I, Lord, send him,' was Hannoch Duke's initial response to an invitation to leave his home in India and go to serve with the United Church of Jamaica and the Cayman Islands. Hannoch, a presbyter of the Church of South India (CSI), was ordained in 1969. Deeply committed to ecumenism and mission, his ministry has included work with young people, the Student Christian Movement in India, workshops, camps and conferences, and being an executive secretary of the Church. His wife Marjorie, at first a teacher of English, was closely involved in the work of the diocese. Most of her working experience has been involved in the considerable social development programmes of the CSI, to meet the needs of some of the poorest in the community. For twenty-seven years she was warden of a working girls' hostel in the Mysore diocese and then, when Hannoch was transferred to the Karnataka diocese, she worked at the Vocational Training Centre, teaching girls with little chance of employment to make things like handbags and industrial gloves so that they can make a living.

Hannoch had almost completed research for a doctorate in theology and was beginning to look for a new challenge when this invitation came from the Council for World Mission (CWM). He and Marjorie did not expect to be asked to go to another part of the world. They hesitated. It was a long way. They did not know anything about Jamaica or anyone there. Deepak, their only son, was in his last year of study for a diploma in technology and they were anxious about his future. At first, Hannoch suggested other ministers who might be approached. But the call from Jamaica was urgent. Bishop Premasagar, then moderator of the CSI, said to him, 'Duke, pack your bags and go!' Marjorie and Hannoch prayed for direction and Hannoch decided to leave his five years' research to respond to God's call. Had they waited another three months, he would have completed his thesis. Underneath the uncertainty, Hannoch was excited at the thought of being called a 'missionary', even though his friends were not so sure. He had grown up with the 'mission concept' and felt he owed much to missionaries from the West who taught and encouraged him.

The churches of the Caribbean suffer a shortage of ministers, not because few men and women come forward for training, but because, once qualified, they are easily attracted by further studies or more prestigious appointments in the United States. The Caribbean churches need help and are asking ministers from other parts of the world to come and serve with them. The United Church would like fifty per cent of ministers in Jamaica to come from other parts of the world to uphold a vision of unity in mission. 'It is a gospel imperative', says Roderick Hewitt, 'that Caribbean Indians should sometimes have an Indian minister.' This was the call that came to Hannoch.

The Council for World Mission is a unique family of thirty partner churches (including the Church of South India, the Presbyterian Church of Wales, and the Congregational Christian Church in Samoa). Although its headquarters is in London, it could as well be in Singapore or Jamaica. Recognizing that all mission is God's, these churches seek to draw closer together as members of Christ's body, sharing hopes and fears, skills and experience, ideas and insights, strengths and weaknesses. By helping in the exchange of long- or short-term missionaries and other types of service, CWM hopes to develop a greater sense of interdependence and involvement of all members in God's mission to the world. Face to face encounters are always the most dynamic way of learning from one another.

Over the last fifteen years, the number of North to South missionaries has dropped, while those coming from South to North and from South to South are increasing. The missionary, who becomes accountable to the host church, is not to be seen as 'filling a gap', but rather as responding to the call, 'Come over and help us'. This is an exciting development and more churches are becoming involved. Usually the sending church covers the cost of preparation and the air fare, and the host church provides financial support equivalent to the stipends of local ministers. Even poorer churches like the Church of Bangladesh want to help in this way.

Hannoch and Marjorie Duke arrived in Jamaica on 15 December 1989 and, after one week's training, Hannoch was given the pastoral care of five churches in Maypen, one of the fastest growing towns in the centre of Jamaica. By the end of his third year, he had established another congregation and opened a sixth church which now has a full-time minister. From her experience of social work in India, Marjorie became fully involved in self-help projects in Maypen. There was plenty to challenge both of them and they knew that they were supported by the gifts and prayers of thirty partner churches around the world.

Jamaicans are very warm, affectionate, friendly people. Hannoch and Marjorie will never forget their welcome and the experience and support of continuing friendships. This helped at times when the transition from an Indian to a Caribbean culture felt hard and painful. At first everything was strange. There were times when, although Hannoch was truly welcome, some of his church families turned for help to Christians of their own culture instead of coming to him. And then he missed the company of men in his rural congregations, but there were plenty of women and children. One third of all households in the Caribbean today are single-parent families, headed by women. Although girls vow to get away from the backbreaking low paid jobs that their mothers did, fifty per cent of women are employed in domestic and agricultural work. Women, both manual labourers and those who have made their way into the professions, are the backbone of church and society in the Caribbean.

The CSI had given Hannoch and Marjorie strong moral values, especially in relation to sexual ethics. The permissiveness of Caribbean life was a distinct culture shock. This open attitude to sex goes back to the early colonial days when marriage was discouraged so that slaves might feel free to breed and produce more slaves. Teenage pregnancy is very common throughout the Caribbean. Some mothers are only twelve years old. After the first baby, a girl may turn to another man for economic support and when he leaves her, she looks for another. Churches in Jamaica are backing the government in Family Life and Family Planning Education, but it seems to Hannoch and Marjorie that sexual misconduct is accepted as a way of life. And this impression is reinforced by the lyrics of popular songs. In the CSI a child born out of wedlock suffers a great stigma. In Jamaica, Hannoch and Marjorie have learnt that no child may be called a bastard. 'What then is sin?' he asks. 'And what does salvation mean in this context?' As a strict evangelical and as a stranger to another culture, Hannoch struggles to find an answer.

Coming from the hierarchical structures of the CSI, Hannoch appreciates the more democratic ethos of the United Church. India is a vast country and the CSI has a membership of over a million and a half, compared to the twenty thousand of the United Church. To turn from the complex structure of the CSI to the intimacy and dialogue of a small church is a refreshing change and so is the spontaneous participation of its members at worship on Sundays. When a preacher quotes a text from the Bible in his sermon, the whole congregation joins in and repeats it after him. There is nothing mechanical about this tradition: it expresses a deep love of God's word. Hannoch likes singing and sometimes in a sermon begins to sing a verse of a hymn and they respond in like manner.

South to South mission is as yet very new, and CWM partner churches are exploring other ways of supporting missionaries like Hannoch and Marjorie. In the past, when CWM was known as the London Missionary Society, recruiting, training, and the support of all missionaries were co-ordinated in Britain. But this is no longer appropriate. How do other churches support their missionaries? Not many CWM member churches have a training programme and are beginning to work out their own guidelines. The needs of an expatriate are different from those of a local minister. Support groups are needed to enable missionaries to understand the culture and expectations of the receiving church, and to help the receiving church to learn from the different spiritual perspectives of their new minister.

From a Jamaican perspective, Hannoch reflects on the number of indigenous missionary societies within India itself and the exchanges of personnel in which they are engaged. Some of them work with the CSI, building up new congregations to hand over to the CSI. 'Every Christian must be taught how to witness to a non-Christian,' say the Friends Missionary Prayer Band which has about three hundred evangelists. For Hannoch, the networking and spirituality of these groups articulate what he would like to see happening on a larger global scale. What prevents mission becoming more global? Yes, there should be more South to South sharing, but the term 'South to South' stuck in his throat. Is there a hint of discrimination in the way we use it, he asks! Certainly within CWM, an increase in South to South exchange is a mark of a new style of mission. The real target is a truly worldwide sharing.

Working for change

MARGARET and ALDO VALLE – Britain to Peru

'I haven't asked for you and I don't need you. You're a foreign missionary. You're backed by a mission agency. But you're a Peruvian and married to a Peruvian. OK. Go and sort out books in the library. . .' Such was the welcome Margaret Valle received from the principal of the theological seminary when she returned to Lima, Peru, in 1990. But the principal soon realized that Margaret was prepared to listen and learn from indigenous Christians, and so accepted and invited her to become college chaplain and share in the training of pastors.

Margaret, who was born in Britain, had a strong conviction that God wanted her to be a 'missionary' and at the age of thirteen, listening to a talk on Peru, she knew where she might be needed. After art school, teacher training and several years at Mount Hermon and the London Bible College, she was sent by a Baptist church in London and the Regions Beyond Missionary Union (RBMU) to Peru in 1959. RBMU sent her into the jungle to share in evangelization and church planting. But on no account was she to form close friendships with Peruvians! When, after two years, she declared her plans to marry Aldo Valle, a Methodist minister, she was asked to leave and told not to return to the area. She would be a bad influence on other missionaries! All reasons given were deeply racist.

Losing all missionary status, Margaret became a national, sharing Aldo's small stipend and bringing up their two adopted children. This was 'real incarnation'—living not on a higher level than the people, but among them, one with them in their poverty.

Marriage across cultures is never easy, but Margaret and Aldo felt brought together as a 'team'. Margaret became deeply involved in the life of the Methodist Church in Peru. But more than that, as a Peruvian wife, she could identify with the suffering of Peruvian women and their need to be valued in a male-dominated society. She began to detect that men are often forced into these roles; this 'macho' image was in fact contrary to their nature and that Christians can challenge this and create a more balanced attitude.

Being a citizen meant she could become actively involved in political life and use her right to vote; to be part of the democratic way of changing things in a society where the poor had been ignored by powerful landowners and a succession of military governments. Even in the 1960s and 70s, violence was increasing. Margaret and Aldo lived in the mountains during these years and news of the real situation was scarce.

In 1979, Margaret returned to Britain with their two teenage children. While they completed their education, she was ordained in 1980 and became minister first in Bradford and then of a multicultural Methodist church in Newham, East London.

Her return to Peru in 1990 symbolized a growing friendship between the Methodist Church in Peru and the British Methodist Church. The Methodist Church in Peru, which has just celebrated its centenary, was founded by the American Methodist Church.

The Communidad Biblica Teologica (CBT), an ecumenical theological college in Lima where she now teaches, is on the 'cutting edge' of society; the only seminary in Peru that overtly encourages students to see the physical needs around them and become involved in the political process. They train men and women of at least twelve different Christian traditions to work alongside the people in their struggle for land, electricity, water, health, education. . . This is part of what it means to be pastors, leaders of church and community in a time of violent change. The seminary is very clear about the need for peaceful demonstrations, denouncing terrorism, but putting pressure on the government and openly denouncing flagrant abuse of human rights. Its staff believe the church is called to a prophetic ministry and to work for reconciliation as well as sensitive evangelism and discipleship.

Through the seminar method of education at CBT, students from widely different social backgrounds are encouraged to work in small groups and listen to one another in the light of their reading of Scripture, sharing insights and relating the Bible to social issues—to live according to biblical principles. Margaret has discovered here that the more church and community move away from hierarchical leadership to learn from the wisdom of indigenous culture, the more their life together is enriched.

Margaret's ministry in Peru also includes pastoral care of a growing congregation in Lima, extension courses in the remoter mountain areas and encouraging the churches there. Terrible poverty and human rights abuses continue; most of the population is underfed. Political changes since 1980 have cost over 25,000 lives—often the mindless killing of innocent Indians, including women and children. Although Peru now has an elected government, violence is perpetrated by terrorist groups who want change on their terms.

There needs to be real change. Although Margaret believes that political structures which deny basic rights are sinful, she also believes that sin comes from within ourselves. We have made or permitted those structures. The good news is that Christ changes people, not souls only, and Christians can then begin to work to change social structures.

But this can be costly. Community and Christian leaders who are seen to work with the poor are caught in the crossfire: suspected by terrorists on one side, and by the government and fellow Christians on the other. Many have been killed or forced to leave the country. Those who struggle for peace and justice risk their lives. 'It costs everything', says Margaret, 'to be a Christian and work for change here in Peru.' One example was Romulo, a much loved and respected Quechua Indian missionary and Bible

translator who openly opposed racism and helped his people
to engage in the struggle for political reform. He was shot.
So was Maria Elena, mayoress of a poor district in Lima,
who had worked with needy families, setting up self-help
groups for women, nutrition programmes, and communal
kitchens. Unafraid, but aware of the risk, she marched
alongside the women in their protests and demands for
better conditions. She was shot by 'Shining Path' terrorists
and her body was dynamited before her family and friends.
Hundreds of other community leaders have been savagely
killed, but thousands more have taken their place. Even the
most peaceful of protests are dispersed by the use of tear
gas and bullets. And church people who are seen 'helping
the poor' are killed. Giving food is interpreted as paternal-
istic and encouraging the poor in bad habits. Some church
and development agencies have had to leave.

Margaret speaks of stark contrasts between terrorists who
exploit people's fear and local Christians whose deep trust
in the power of God to bring in the Kingdom transcends all
bitterness. They read the Scriptures and act. Their acceptance of the direction in which the Spirit leads them has
helped her to grow in faith and trust in the power of Christ
to heal and reconcile. She could not have survived without
this. And here lies the crucial role of the church in Peru
today: that of 'bridge builder'. The government doesn't
want to talk, and terrorists refuse. Only the church has
within itself the potential to build up the community and
work for a future in which men, women, and children can
live together in peace and help people to trust one another
and communicate again.

Yet Margaret sees the context of her work extending far
beyond Peru. In a letter in 1992, she described the Columbus
celebration as 'a time for serious reflection, repentance,
confession, and a call for restitution for the awful suffering it caused and still causes. I feel that much of the terrible
violence in this dirty war is not so much a class struggle,
but is caused by the deep racism left as a legacy by the
European invaders.' She tells of times when, conscious of

mistakes made by well-intentioned Christians with 'colonial attitudes', she has felt ashamed that she too is white.

Both missionaries and other European visitors to Latin America must leave behind the baggage of their culture, she says, and 'travel light'. Missionaries are still needed as fellow Christians and encouragers, but they must be critical of attitudes with which they have grown up. They are needed not only for what they can give, but for what they can learn from those to whom they go. That would help to change things in Britain too!

Witnessing for Christ in a divided country

LUIS and ESTELA BALDEON – Peru to Ireland

Luis was minister of a congregation in a very poor area of Lima, the capital of Peru, where ordinary people cope with the daily realities of overpopulation, unemployment, and terrorism. Until he came there, the church at Comas had dwindled to nine members, but Luis gathered them together to hear his vision of sharing Christ with this community. Beginning with lapsed members, they set goals and began visiting families, inviting them to church. They started a Sunday school and visited the homes of children who came, not primarily to evangelize but to get to know and befriend them. With the help of other churches in Lima, a carpentry workshop was opened to enable boys to develop skills for employment. Before entering the ministry, Luis had been a lawyer and was still a member of the Association of

Professional Evangelical Lawyers, so he was able to advise single mothers in matters of legal aid and to help others to know their rights. In addition to his degree in law, Luis has degrees in education and theology and was involved in teaching and lecturing as well as fulfilling the usual tasks of a minister.

Estela, who is Japanese, worked with the Methodist Women's Association, raising money to provide milk for street children and sheets for the children's ward at the local hospital. Out of her deep concern for social issues and love of people, Estela encouraged women in their neighbour-hood to start up home industries and begin to improve the quality of life for themselves and their children. There was more than enough to occupy both of them and the Comas congregation was growing rapidly.

But 'God moves in a mysterious way': an invitation came from the Irish Methodist Conference through MCOD's World Church in Britain and Ireland programme, which invites ministers and their families to come and serve in Britain or Ireland for a period of five years. It wasn't long before Luis was introducing himself, Estela, and their children: Toshio, Naomi, Jarumi and Yumi, to Greencastle Methodist Church in the suburbs of Belfast. The environment was different, their grasp of the English language felt hopelessly inadequate, but they were fully accepted and welcomed and the gospel was the same.

Luis said, 'We came here bringing the message of Jesus Christ. This message is everlasting and up to date in every place and in any time. Though we come from far away lands, God is in that place too, caring for and loving His children. For Him there are no boundaries of culture, age, language, background, or sex. He is our Father who pours on every people and every nation His love, for . . . you are all one in Christ.'

Luis, though small in physical stature, has a dynamic, warm, friendly personality, and his sense of humour and spontaneity quickly win people's friendship and lift their spirits. 'I am a Belfast man!' he says, or 'I am an Ulster

man!' He will tell you that the strengths of his ministry are
pastoral care and evangelism. He began by setting goals, as
he had done in Lima. 'I want to see a living and growing
church,' he says. Much of his time is spent visiting members,
those on the fringe of the church and many who have no
links with it. Through his preaching and articles in local
papers and magazines, he shows what is central to his ministry: a personal experience of Jesus Christ as Saviour in
whom alone the church lives and grows. This message stems
from his own experience. Although a lifelong Methodist,
the presence of Christ only became real to him when, at
home in Peru, he was involved in a serious car crash and
had to undergo complicated surgery. He became acutely
aware of his mortality and complete dependence on God. A
sense of the closeness of Jesus and the prayers of fellow
Christians changed his life and led to his being called to
the ministry.

The congregation at Greencastle is growing. Casual
worshippers come more regularly. There are many new
members, non-Christians are beginning to come to worship, and a greater social awareness is developing. 'God
sent them to us,' comments one member. 'We have been
touched by Luis and Estela's ministry.' And by the children
too—especially as the family has adopted one couple in the
congregation as 'Grandpa and Gramma'. Their lives have
been profoundly challenged by their close relationship
with this caring, open and affectionate family. Everyone
receives hugs from all the family on Sundays, both when
they arrive at church and before they return home. 'The
children's manners are impeccable,' they say. 'And they
always have a smile.'

Birthdays and baptisms are particularly important. Many
members get a phone call on their birthday—reminding
them that they are members of God's family; they are
important to God.

Luis's 'availability'—to old and young alike—and regular
pastoral visiting have been greatly appreciated and many
are deeply moved when, after hearing their news, he kneels

and prays with them. When he visits someone in hospital, he doesn't just go to the church member he has come to see, but goes round the ward with a word for everyone. When he conducts a funeral, he takes care of every detail and communicates a genuine sharing of the family's grief.

The Baldeons have also made Peru real to the people of Greencastle. Peru, the third largest country of South America, is no longer just a name on the map. When opportunities arise, the family love to tell of its majestic snow-capped Andean mountains, the well-irrigated valleys, rich farmlands, vegetation, variety of animals and insect life, and through it all comes their sense of wonder at the presence of the creator God. They share the pain and problems of their people: the unemployment, poor housing and health facilities. One out of every ten babies never reaches the age of five. These facts are no longer cold statistics, but are about real people; friends and compatriots of the Baldeons. They share the frustration of a country rich in natural resources, with a strong potential to support and feed its people, but burdened by the high rates of interest they have to pay on loans made to them by western banks in the 1970s. Debt and interest repayments by developing countries, like Peru, amount to three times what they receive in aid.

But the Baldeons have also to relate to the situation in Northern Ireland, witnessing to Christ in a divided country. Many have expressed concern about their personal safety, but Luis replies with examples of much greater danger at the hands of terrorists in Peru. As an 'outsider', he can go into the homes of people in Northern Ireland whom local priests and ministers dare not go near. Having been a lawyer in Peru, he is not afraid to talk with police and to enter situations where people have been victims of violence. His sensitivity makes him welcome in both Protestant and Catholic pulpits. Reflecting on his Peruvian experience, he knows he has learnt of God's power in times of human weakness and anguish and that the church can only offer a ministry of reconciliation 'if it is simultaneously fed with spiritual bread'.

Some members of the church at Greencastle speak very movingly of how they have been 'humbled' by all they have received from the Baldeons. 'We did not know what to expect.' They tell of the initial shock when they knew they were to have a minister from Peru. But now, as they look back, they recognize the movement of God in bringing them together and giving them an entirely new way of looking at their place in God's mission to the world. They thought they would never be able to understand someone who wasn't used to preaching in English and whose accent was different. But they found that made them listen all the more carefully. They have been enriched in ways they never dreamt would happen. 'We have been brought closer to God,' they say, and speak of their 'tremendous sense of indebtedness to God' for such an opportunity to see 'the love of Christ in action'.

And coming to Ireland has been for both Luis and Estela another opportunity to grow in faith, to rely more and more upon God, and to experience the breadth of God's love through the welcome given by another part of the world Church.

A time to be silent

SIMON and JULIA HILL – Britain to Malaŵi

Simon and Julia Hill had trained as history teachers and wondered if they might be used overseas (Simon had already spent two years teaching in Zimbabwe, following graduation). After writing to a number of organizations, they were offered a two year contract by USPG to serve with the Anglican Church in Malaŵi. In September 1990 they

arrived at Malosa Secondary School, on a magnificent
wooded hillside not far from the Mozambique border.
From the beginning, Simon and Julia sensed a warmth of
welcome and the general happiness and spontaneity of
the people. They were overwhelmed by the beauty of God's
creation and the joy of being in a country 'where God is
so freely acknowledged as a part of people's daily lives'.

Another overwhelming first impression was the tremendous thirst for education. Students are selected for secondary
education by a national examination in their last year at
primary school. Like most African secondary schools,
Malosa was a boarding school, though so short of accommodation that some pupils had to share beds or sleep on the
floor. They came from different parts of the country and
from different religious traditions.

Subjects studied included maths, English, Chichewa (the
national language), physical science, biology, geography,
history, commerce and Bible knowledge (which all students
were expected to attend, including Muslims, even though
they represented thirty per cent of the population). Simon
and Julia taught mostly history and English with some maths
and Bible knowledge. The history and geography syllabus
focused first on Africa and then broadened out to look at
the rest of the world. Each day, lessons started at 7.00 a.m.
and ended at 3.20 p.m. There were four year groups to the
Malawian Certificate of Education (the equivalent of GCSE)
with external examinations at the end of the second and
fourth years (Malawi has its own examination board). Some
went on to university, the polytechnic or to agricultural
college. For fourth-year leavers, employment prospects
were grim. Life in Malawi is unpredictable, and careerism
a luxury of the few. Simon and Julia became acutely aware
of their 'accident of birth'. Seeing people who were as
intelligent as themselves, but who had few opportunities
to use their skills, reminded them of their own privilege,
security, and education.

There were few classroom disciplinary problems, though
pressures to succeed often led to cheating in examinations.

Students were mostly polite and hard-working. Many asked for extra work! Problems did however arise: bullying, occasional drunkenness, pregnancies. . . In Africa, pupils tend to be older than their counterparts in English schools. They may begin late, or drop out for a year or two, for lack of funds. Or they may have to keep repeating their final year at primary level until one of the limited places at secondary schools becomes available. Only about four per cent of the population receive a secondary education.

Malosa had a chapel which was used for Sunday worship and for services during the week. Roman Catholics, members of the Presbyterian Church of Central Africa, Seventh Day Adventists, and Anglicans all used it. Most weekdays, young people themselves led prayers. Simon and Julia were aware of 'something deep within' their students, giving expression to commitment, trust, and openness. There was a natural spirituality. Africans do not compartmentalize religious feelings and thoughts, but allow them to enter into everything they do.

Having been sent by a mission agency meant being under the authority of the bishop of the Anglican Church in Malaŵi. The headmaster of the school was also a Malawian and so were most of the staff. Simon and Julia welcomed this, and were aware that how they lived and responded to everyday issues mattered to both church and school. Realizing that countries like Malaŵi had experienced too many arrogant westerners going out 'to show them the way', they were determined to resist getting sucked into an 'expat' ghetto. They wanted to work with Malawians and learn from them. This required flexibility. They might have learnt more efficient ways of running a school in Britain, but in Malaŵi they learnt that 'efficiency without happy relationships is not worth having'. Disagreements were not dealt with in a confrontational way. In Africa, relationships are everything.

And being away from Britain, they discovered a sense of proportion about what they had left behind. They began to appreciate the insignificance of possessions, especially

when people with very little came with gifts of food and
welcomed them in their homes. An African meal can always
be stretched to bring others into the circle. They were
humbled when older women knelt to thank them for something and were deeply moved by unashamed wailing at the
death of relatives or friends—an overt African expression of
solidarity in grief.

Simon and Julia's marriage was sometimes a focus of
discussion. African tradition, for example, gives pride of
place to men, while women literally bear the burdens.
Their students were surprised that Julia allowed Simon
to get up first in the morning and to carry her books and
cases! On one occasion, much to their amusement, Julia
brought a history lesson to an end with, 'I really must finish.
Mr Hill will have cooked the lunch!' There was much to
learn from one another and plenty to laugh about. When
their students finally bid them farewell, they said, 'We
shall miss you because you've smiled.' 'It was sad', said
Julia, 'that we were given credit for something so basic.'

They became aware of enormous national problems:
debt, inflation, the devaluation of currency, suppression of
political dissidents, drought. . . They recall a flood which
killed hundreds and made thousands homeless, and another
which brought chaos to the school: mud sliding down the
hillside, blocking the dam on which their water supply
depended. Yet another downpour caused a landslide on
the mountain behind the school, washing away precious
topsoil. Malawians called such landslides 'Napolo', 'a
snake coming down the mountainside to kill them'. A few
hundred miles away were the overcrowded villages of
Mozambique refugees (almost ten per cent of Malaŵi's
population). Vehicles of Save the Children Fund and
UNHCR were often seen distributing food.

Perhaps the most difficult aspect of their life in Malaŵi
was to be aware of political conflicts, recognizing that as
expatriates they had no right to voice an opinion. Malaŵi
is a one-party state. For years, no one dared to speak out
against the government until the first Sunday in Lent 1992,

when, in all Roman Catholic churches, a pastoral letter
from the bishops was read. It touched a number of issues:
equality, AIDS, freedom of speech, problems in education. . . 'Nobody should ever have to suffer reprisals for
honestly expressing and living up to their convictions—
intellectual, religious or political.' They went on to say that
fear of harassment and mutual suspicion breed a society in
which the gifts and skills of its people are not used for the
common good. They called on every citizen to work for
change. This is 'not only right; it is a duty'.

It was immediately declared by the government a seditious
document. Anyone possessing a copy had to hand it in to
the nearest police station. The bishops were interrogated by
the police and kept under house arrest. In the Malawian
press they were accused of 'flouting' freedom of worship.
Leading party members demanded their death. All public
worship was from this moment scrutinized. The Good
Friday procession in Simon and Julia's local (Chichewa)
church was forbidden. Many Christians were afraid to discuss
the matter, even in their own homes, for fear of informers.
There were riots and student demos. The university was
closed. The political structures and Malaŵi's appalling
human rights record led to the international community
suspending all non-humanitarian aid.

But the church was not silenced. Some Presbyterian
ministers got together and demanded the release of the
bishops, and were imprisoned too. Then an ecumenical
team from outside the country came in to express solidarity
and the government was forced to take notice. What is even
more encouraging—because a few men were prepared to
suffer to say what others dared not voice—the political
process is beginning to change. As in most one-party
States, news of these events was suppressed within the
country. Simon and Julia, who were full of admiration
for what the Catholic bishops had done, heard most of it
on BBC World Service. But whatever their feelings or
opinions, they could only listen: they were not able to
discuss the issues with their students.

Simon and Julia returned to Britain in August 1992. Their
contract had come to an end and USPG had decided not to
replace them. This was partly due to financial restraints, but
also to a reluctance to continue sending expatriate staff.
While at a policy level this sounds right, it was hard for
Simon and Julia. There being no guarantee that they would
be replaced by Malawians, they felt as though they were
abandoning their students.

Simon is now a student at Oxford, preparing for ordination as a priest of the Anglican Church and Julia is teaching
at a comprehensive school in Bicester. Whether they will go
overseas again is an open question, but there is one thing
they are sure of—and that is that they gained so much from
this experience in Malaŵi—their lives will never be the same
again. Wherever they go in the future, they will want to
share with others a sense of belonging to the world Church.

Building bridges of understanding

SARAH ATTEWELL – Britain to China

There is a character in the Chinese language meaning
'love', which you will find displayed in many churches
in China. 'That is where you begin,' says Sarah Attewell.
'There are so many barriers in China, but without love,
you won't get past them. In Europe you can argue a point,
but in China it's different.'

In China, missionaries are not welcome and evangelism
is officially forbidden. Sarah went to China in 1989 as a
teacher for the Amity Foundation. It all began in 1985
when, recovering from a serious illness, she made a deeper
commitment to God, little realizing how far it would take

her! She returned to her job as personnel manager for BT International, but, feeling challenged to do something different, registered for a six-week Teaching English as a Foreign Language (TEFL) course. Some students were preparing to work in other countries like Germany and Japan. When they asked, 'What are you going to do, Sarah?' she had to admit that she had not looked beyond the course itself. And then China seemed to lodge itself in her mind. Her mother had mentioned that English teachers were needed there and Sarah had come to know two Chinese students on the course and was fascinated by them. Suddenly it became clear. A friend gave her some information about the Amity Foundation and she sent in an application, but was too late to go that year. So she remained another two and a half years teaching English at a language school in Woking but when the call to China persisted, she applied to Amity again.

The Amity Foundation is an independent voluntary organization set up by Chinese Christians to promote health, education, rural development, and social services for their people, and to make Christian participation in community building more widely known to them. As they help communities to help themselves, they use mostly Chinese people. The largest programme is in teaching English—the language of trade and commerce. Teachers from English-speaking countries are invited to help mainly in rural teachers' colleges and smaller universities which have limited funding. Sarah was sent to teach at the Jiangsu Polytechnic University by the side of the River Yangtse and just five miles from the town of Zhenjiang, near Nanjing.

Although she had been well prepared for what she would face in China, her first impressions were of a very alien environment: crowded buses, people pushing and shoving, abruptness in shops, dirty streets . . . all so different from what she had visualized, and so was the culture. 'It seemed as though you had to do everything upside down!' she said. Everything she did and everywhere she went seemed to be approached by a circuitous route, and often there was no one to consult. It seemed unfathomable. How could she work in this strange environment and why did God bring her here? It was a real challenge and the first lesson she learnt was patience.

Sarah arrived just after the Tiananmen Square episode. Everything was tense. The Chinese did not know what would happen next or how the economy would be affected. Many overseas businesses had pulled out. People were afraid to talk about it, especially to foreigners and feared to be seen with them. All this made Sarah's first year very hard. The university staff, however, anxious that they might have to make do without expatriate help, was pleased to see her and gave her a good welcome. She was given a pleasant apartment in the guest house with her own balcony. The only snag was that the compound gates were locked at 10.00 p.m., an hour earlier than the students had to be in! Sarah and an American student, Ann Stuart, were the only expatriates on the staff for the first year. Although this accentuated their sense of loneliness, it forced them to socialize with Chinese students and colleagues. They soon found themselves helping others to get to know the Chinese. Each year the university hosted a group of twelve students from places like Trinidad, Ghana, Equador, and Uganda. They were older than the Chinese students, found the food unpalatable, and missed their families left at home. Sarah and Ann valued their friendship.

Before she went to China, Sarah had been a member of a large evangelical Anglican church which had given her a strong foundation of faith and teaching. With deep gratitude, she found this helped to sustain her through the most difficult traumas of settling into this strange environment. And, in her initial sense of isolation, she came closer to God, her only resource to cope with daily anxieties. One day, when life was at its worst, she sat down and wrote a letter to God, expressing frustration that God had brought her there and all the anxieties, large and small, even her fear of losing a filling and having to go to a Chinese dentist! Those were her prayers and she put them away. About the same time, a foreign affairs officer brought her an old copy of an American missionary magazine, on the back of which was a colourful picture of tulips. There are very few visuals in China; everything is drab and this picture, which she placed on her wall, was a sign of hope—and so was its text from Isaiah 58, reminding her that God is like a spring 'whose waters never fail'. These words from a Jewish exile of 2,500 years ago spoke directly to Sarah and remained with her for the rest of her time in China.

She taught English language and conversation, literature, listening skills and background to Britain—which comprised anything and everything about life at home—travel, work, the British weekend. . . Students were friendly, hardworking, lively, and had a great sense of humour. They were so keen to learn about Britain, she hardly knew where to begin! Undergraduates were much easier to teach—they had to score high marks in English to qualify for the course—and she had a favourite second-year class which she taught for ten hours a week. Postgraduates were older and, because their training in English was more in the past, lacked confidence to write and speak in English, and Sarah had to begin by teaching them the basics. They came in small groups of three or four which made a pleasant change from larger classes and, because they were nearer her own age, became good friends. Sometimes she was expected to deliver a lecture to a packed lecture theatre of about three hundred and fifty students on a subject of general interest like 'Improving Fast Reading'.

Although not obliged to learn the language, Sarah learnt a considerable amount from a Chinese friend before she went. She wanted to get to know people quickly and make friends. In Zhenjiang, she had weekly lessons from a Chinese teacher who could speak no English! Their conversations about everyday things increased Sarah's understanding of the Chinese way of life.

One of her greatest achievements was learning to cook for herself—to go to the market and select strange foods and come back and cook something that was edible! Well into her second year, she recognized how much she had adapted:

'Walking past a fish tank one day and gazing idly at the colourful, lively occupant, I caught myself wondering, "Hmm. . . What would that taste like?" '

Although she was able to do some sightseeing in the vacations, Sarah felt it was important, during the term, to stay in and around the campus at weekends and spend time with people. Chinese friendships became a real joy. Their hospitality was overwhelming. As she made more friends, she came to realize that she was beginning to understand their culture. 'It was a privilege', she said, 'to be part of a community for two years. I was made welcome and received far more than I gave.'

Sometimes she worshipped at the large well-attended church in Zhenjiang, but more often went to the village church near the university. The congregation of about forty-five people was quite elderly, but included some young families who were eager to get to know Sarah. She was both comforted by all their greetings and encouraged by their commitment. There was a sense of hope. They were glad to be there. Above all, there was an absence of denominationalism. It belonged to the mainstream Three Self Church which Amity encourages its workers to support and which, as one church, replaced the many denominations that existed before the Cultural Revolution. It is a growing church. In 1989 there were 200,000 converts, bringing the total of Protestant Christians in China to almost six million people. By the end of 1989 over 7,000 churches had opened, of which more than 3,000 were new ones. In 1993 the total number of Protestant Christians in China was estimated to be between six and nine million. Being a member of the Three Self Church throughout her two years, Sarah learnt that it is possible for Christians to overcome their differences and worship together. The pastors, who were either very elderly or just graduated from theological college, preached very biblical sermons about how to live a Christian life. In some areas, the Religious Affairs Bureau—a government department—exercises strict control over the activities and teachings of the local church; and evangelism, which includes work with children, is forbidden.

Sarah learnt from the spiritual strength of elderly members who had remained faithful during the years of the Cultural Revolution. Many highly educated Christians had been separated from husbands, wives, and children to do manual work in factories. Yet there was no bitterness; they were radiant, loving people.

For Sarah and her friends, the lifestyle was simple and, living five miles away from the town, people were their only resource; they had to make their own entertainment most of the time. The Chinese love stories and they spent much time storytelling, making music, playing chess and badminton (without nets). Sarah learnt that much of what we take for granted in the West, we can live without. 'When you come down to basics', she said, 'the same fundamental things are important to people, wherever they are: family life, a satisfying role and the ability to sustain oneself and one's family. This is where our joys and sorrows are centred.' In comparison, the concept of 'upward mobility' is peripheral. The Chinese understanding of time taught her to set work aside to help someone with a problem. When students were sick, other students worked in shifts to look after and cook for them.

As bridges of understanding formed, preconceptions were swept away. Many students had been conditioned into thinking that western teachers were indoctrinated by their governments and acted like automatons. Others, although they said little, had started to question whether the Chinese government was acting in the best interests of the people, especially since Tiananmen Square. China has a very materialistic philosophy. Students seemed to be aware of a vacuum within themselves that they could not fill. Sometimes questions about faith arose quite naturally out of, for example, a reference to a christening in a reading text on the topic of family reunions. Although it was impossible to know what effect they had on students, Sarah and other expatriate teachers felt that their presence did something to satisfy the feeling of emptiness. Only the bad influences of the West were presented and attacked by the media. Everyone, especially young people, is fascinated by the West, absorbing everything western they can—the good and the bad. Sarah felt their role as teachers was to be honest about negative aspects while striving to offer a more accurate picture than the Chinese media, but also to encourage students not to accept everything western without questioning underlying values.

Since returning to Britain in 1991, Sarah taught for the first year and then took up an appointment with World Vision, recruiting staff to work on their overseas programmes. In China, she had developed a keen interest in Amity's agricultural and community development work, and started to understand some of the problems of developing countries. She wanted to identify with that kind of work.

Sarah went to China to work with people in their need, sharing the life of the community and, through her way of life, communicating something about God's love. In her room hung a poster that displayed the Chinese character for 'love'. Underneath it was written the definition of love in 1 Corinthians 13. She was greatly surprised and deeply moved one day, when a student came in to have a cup of tea and read it slowly and carefully. Then he looked up and said, 'That's like you!'

New ways of being 'a church'

MAGALI DO NASCIMENTO CUNHA and CLAUDIO RIBEIRO – Brazil to Britain

Magali Cunha was born in Rio de Janeiro City in 1963, a year before the military dictatorship took over. It was a time of repression and the persecution of many who were working for a better country, one more episode in the saga of five hundred years of oppression for the peoples of Latin America and their struggle for justice. The new government said they would develop the country, open the doors for international commerce and bring in the 'modernity of the First World'. Many ordinary people supported their goal. At school, Magali was taught to hate the past, her people's traditions and culture, the old-fashioned, colonialism and all that, and think of the future the new government would build.

Some years before, her parents had come from the countryside into the city, looking for a better life. They met there and married. It was a hard life. Her father worked in the harbour carrying heavy boxes and her mother became a domestic. But they were able to provide a better quality of life and education for their two children. And they taught them to be critical of what they learnt at school. 'Look around you,' her father said. 'What do you see? Do our neighbours enjoy the benefits of world trade? Modernity is for the privileged few; it is not for the majority of Brazilians. . .' This informal education at home influenced her choice to go to university and study journalism, to help her people to learn the truth, to struggle for their rights and liberate themselves.

As a family, they were nominal Catholics, but when Magali was thirteen, her mother became a member of the

Methodist church and Magali was introduced to a youth fellowship. This was an interesting time to learn about 'church'. The Methodist Church in Brazil, which had been established by the American Methodist Church, was modelled according to their structures. But it was not growing because it did not have a Brazilian identity. It was not responding to Brazilian needs. Magali became part of her church's process of reflection and discussion—how should the church respond to reality? With other teenagers, she was encouraged to think about her roots and discovered much that she was not taught at school. She learnt to be proud of the indigenous culture and those who gave their lives for democracy. And, instead of trying to worship a God far away in heaven, she learnt that God was in their struggles, supporting them in very concrete ways, challenging them to share God's will of happiness and good life for all. This was a turning-point in her life. At the same time, the Roman Catholic Church and other Protestant Churches were discovering the way of Base Christian Communities.

After university, she decided not to work for a national paper or magazine, where her writing would be filtered by 'powerful people', but to find an alternative way to help the grassroots of society. She was invited to work for the Ecumenical Centre for Documentation and Information in Rio City, helping to organize seminars and workshops, and publishing magazines, books, videos, and newspapers for church groups in Brazil.

Then came the second turning-point in her life: her marriage to Claudio, a minister in Baixada, a very poor part of Rio. Magali's family had been poor, but they had had a good life and been shielded from the degree of poverty that faced her here. Abandoned by the government, one hospital served eight cities. There was a complete lack of basic facilities, and child mortality was a daily reality. And few churches could afford a minister. Claudio, who also worked for the Ecumenical Centre of Documentation and Information, was involved part-time with a project to provide pastors for this area, and also to empower lay people to work without a minister. Magali helped, organizing seminars to help them understand the needs and see how they could respond and move forward as a church. They were people of strong faith and great initiative, and she found herself learning with them—learning how people with so little can be ready for God's mission. This was another process of 'conversion'.

It was at this stage that staff of MCOD were visiting Brazil, heard about her and invited her to Britain as a 'Partner in Mission' for one year to work with 'Grassroots', a new ecumenical programme, set up by Christian Aid, CAFOD, MCOD, USPG, and other agencies. Twenty-nine years old, Magali came in a spirit of openness, ready to do anything, bringing journalistic and workshop skills. Although her English was good, she welcomed the six-weeks' language course at Selly Oak to gain confidence and to learn something about the British way of life before she embarked on the programme for which she had been invited.

According to what she had been taught in Brazil, everything in Britain was wonderful! But both church and society were in crisis. Magali saw the recession at its worst—'consequences of a capitalist regime—ordinary people who had come to rely on a standard of life they might never have again'. And the church was bemoaning the problems of decreasing membership . She soon realized that British people need to hear about liberation too!

'Grassroots' is an ecumenical programme offering cross-cultural teams to churches and groups of churches, to work for a weekend with twenty to thirty Christians who may be able to make a commitment to carry forward its vision and method. It is based on the Latin American experience of Base Christian Communities, and the Catholic and Protestant emphasis on God's option for the poor. It challenges passivity, and encourages participatory learning and the importance of the Bible as springboards for action.

For a whole year, Magali led teams and met with church groups of different traditions. She began by getting everyone to tell their 'story', not merely a 'getting to know you' exercise, but preparing them to listen to other people's stories, to learn from someone of another culture, to identify ways of responding to local issues, to deepen spirituality and see what it means to be 'a church'.

Coming from Brazil, where they have struggled to involve the people, churches here seemed very formal, very centred on the minister or priest. In Brazil many lay people play a more active role than the minister. In Grassroots weekends here, she encouraged people to do things informally and discover a new spontaneity, ways of bringing their daily life to the life of the church. In Brazil, she had learnt that the church is not a building, but a group of people come together to learn of God: to study the Bible together, pray, worship and learn how to respond to the needs of the community. The church has a mission to share the good news that God's Kingdom of peace, justice, and love is possible, and we can build it together.

The aim of mission in Britain, she says, is not to fill churches. 'It doesn't matter whether people come to church or not, but that the church is going to people in their struggle. In Britain, people spend all their time discussing if they're going to repair the roof and if they are going to have pews or chairs! Brazil has buildings too, but they are not the main thing. The church is community and this is what needs building here: being able to respond, not just to what's going on in Bosnia, but in the next street! Brazil is still reflecting and learning and this is a process that needs to be learnt here.'

Grassroots is enabling those who are 'developed' to change, and there are signs of hope in Britain. Here and there Magali discovered groups of people who were willing to be 'church' in a new way. She found among them an openness to learn from herself and others in her team; to learn from their struggle and find an energy to begin again. Most came to these weekends expecting to hear stories about Brazil, but found themselves identifying with the Brazilian mind and stirred from their complacency by her biblical insights. Magali has remarkable gifts to lead, to involve people in worship, and to create 'community'. In a short space of time, they grew in faith and went away profoundly challenged—'gob-smacked', one of them remarked! 'A breath of fresh air', said others.

Magali and Claudio returned to Brazil in August 1993 to carry on with their work for the Ecumenical Centre and their ministry to the *fluminense* (those born in the State of Rio) in Baixada. 1993 is the tenth anniversary of work in that area. Reflecting on all that happened in their year in Britain, Magali recognized ways in which they had grown. This was the first time they had been away from Brazil and, for the first four months, she was without Claudio. Claudio was granted a sabbatical to come for eight months, to study at the Selly Oak colleges and to be with Magali. He went with her to share in some of the Grassroots weekends and other conferences. 'You come from a situation completely different from your own and you learn from it,' Magali said. 'You are enriched by the faith of others.' It was an opportunity to look back on her work at home and understand, to give value to things she hadn't recognized before and discover new priorities.

And it was a time of renewed faith. Even in Brazil, Magali had heard about European churches closing for lack of members. It was useful to experience this, and talk with people about signs of hope, and learn together to see the other side of the crisis. 'You can be a Christian wherever you are,' she said. 'God is the same, in Brazil and here. But we have to be open to listen to what God is saying in different contexts. God's word of liberation, which was given to the Israelites in Egypt, doesn't change. All who are 'imprisoned' in a British context can experience it.' She still has that vision of God's mission she found with the group of teenagers in her home church—that the experience of the Kingdom is possible for all. She wrote for the International Bible Reading Association:

> This should be the beauty of the mission of the church: the church being able to dream and encourage others to

do the same, believing that this new world is possible, the Kingdom is possible and the good news can be made concrete through our attitudes of love and fellowship.

On her passport, she was described as 'a missionary'. Yet she didn't see herself in any way special. 'In Brazil, every Christian is a missionary! You can be a missionary in your own neighbourhood,' she said. 'I bring an experience from Brazil but the experience people have here is just as important.' Magali came as a 'Partner in Mission'. Do we invite a 'partner' to go around talking about 'My work in Brazil' or to contribute to and challenge the life of our church? Do we dwell only on those reasons why we should give to support mission in other parts of the world, or open our minds to learn from ways in which God is revealed to others? Magali recognized 'the Spirit moving us to both give and receive'. How ready are we to be influenced and make the changes others enable us to see? How genuine is our sense of partnership?

A shared struggle

JANE ELLA MONTENEGRO –

Philippines to Britain

Bless your people, Lord,
who have walked too long in this night of pain.
For the child has no more tears to cry
and the old people no song of joy to sing,
and the blood of our youth drains away in the gutters.
The cry from the cross is heard throughout our land.

The pain in your nailed hands is carried by the worker.
Terrible thirst is in the mouth of the farmer,
too many women mourn the loss of their sons,
and all the earth is turned into another calvary.
With your spirit, Lord, we cry for peace.
With your spirit, Lord, we struggle to be free.

A prayer from PENTECOST, a church-based organization, quoted in the 14th Biennial Convention Resource Book of the National Council of Churches of the Philippines in 1989.

'How can the people begin to pray within the community instead of in the church?' Through the life and witness of Filipino Base Christian Communities, people are beginning to discover the answer. But this pertinent question came from Christians in one of the poorest housing estates in Britain during the visit of Jane Ella Montenegro, a representative of the United Church of Christ in the Philippines.

Having left behind the complex problems of her country, Jane's first culture shock as she entered Britain in the summer of 1993 was its prevailing affluence and wastefulness. The inequality between homes filled with possessions here and the depleting natural resources of Third World countries filled her with anger. And people in Britain seemed unable even to articulate their faith, including those who attend Mass daily. Where was God in all this? Gradually, through the warm and welcoming friendship of those who invited her, she said her rage melted and was replaced by 'openness, vulnerability, and objectivity'. And then she began to feel for the marginalized people of Britain, where the gap between, not only rich and poor, but middle income and poor has widened considerably in the last decade. She was taken to housing estates managed by local authorities in which two-thirds of the population depend on state benefit and over half are one-parent families. Evidence of vandalism, graffiti, boarded-up deserted flats, litter, and fear of violence added to people's sense of isolation, abandonment, and alienation from the rest of British society.

Ecumenical teams and groups of monks and nuns have

been taking initiatives to build Christian community within some of these estates, where, although most people feel alienated from the Church, about two-thirds of them admit to having some faith. How then can they be helped to articulate that faith in community? What is there to celebrate and give thanks for anyway?

To try to find the answer to some of these questions, the Philippine Ecumenical Network (PEN) set up a project to invite two Filipino lay liturgists who have worked with Base Christian Communities in their own context to spend some time in this country working with the 'concrete grassroots' to develop lay liturgies. Jane Montenegro, who works with the Office of the Laity of the United Church of Christ in the Philippines, was one of the two invited. A programme for the empowerment of the laity has been developed in this decade towards participatory lay liturgy. Even in the Roman Catholic Church, it is not uncommon to find fifty or more Base Christian Communities in one diocese.

PEN, supported by a number of mission and development agencies like CAFOD, Christian Aid, USPG, CMS, and others, came together in 1988 to explore ways in which the Filipino experience can help 'to create opportunities for mutual exchange between Filipino Christians and Christians in this country who are trying to link their personal struggle for social justice with a celebration of their faith'.

The aims of the PEN liturgy project were to help British groups to think through how they can 'meet people's need for worship and religious celebration'; to establish contact between groups in the Philippines and groups in Britain who are 'marginalized from the mainstream of society as well as from church life'; and to create opportunities for mutual support in the struggle towards personal and social transformation.

From an early age, Jane Montenegro became aware of the struggles of her people and began to reflect and ask the question: Why? Jane's father was a minister of the United Church of Christ in the Philippines, a union of the Reformed, Lutheran, Anabaptist, and Episcopal traditions.

She remembers their house being stoned and her father running from a firebrand for preaching Christ. Her mother worked as a nurse with a logging company hospital, and Jane watched and felt pain as the mountains were stripped of trees, and rivers where she played turned brown. Why was it happening? At the same time, friends aged thirteen and fourteen were getting married. Within five years they had four or five children and began to look old. Why? She learnt how men, who lived away from their families in the provinces to work with logging companies on the mountains, turned to prostitution. And she knew of women, many of them in their early teens, who sold their bodies to feed their families. Why? 'This was not in our culture,' she said. 'It was exported to us.'

Jane questioned the structures of society that kept people poor, and the corruption of those in power. She was deeply influenced by student activists. When she became a public school teacher, she became involved in communicating labour rights. People had to be taught what was going on and to know their rights, especially with the declaration of martial law in 1972, in the time of President Marcos. Very soon the mountain ranges where she grew up had been militarized and became known as the 'Killing Fields' of Surigao Sur. People lived in constant fear of harassment. Any crops they produced were easy prey to the heavily armed military. Any who came near were suspected as spies, rebels, or subversives. The Philippines' human rights records can testify to this.

During her five-week visit to Britain, Jane stayed in the parishes of Hartcliffe and Withywood on the edge of Bristol, the Ladywood estate in Birmingham, the Heathtown estate in Wolverhampton and Bethnal Green in East London—all areas of great disaffection and alienation, where many residents would prefer not to live. Within each district, ecumenical, catalyst groups are active and already creating their own liturgies. Jane's itinerary was planned in consultation with them.

Jane's approach, through conversation and informal

sharing, was to begin where the people were and to affirm
what they had become. On her first evening in Heathtown,
a multiracial community, for example, she asked those who
came to introduce themselves and say something good
about their community, something that might be worth
celebrating. They spoke of 'a high degree of acceptance', 'a
lot of tolerance of each other', 'a sense of community', 'a
shared struggle', 'an extraordinary sense of mutual support'.
In Hartcliffe one woman who had lived there for thirty-
nine years felt so deeply that she belonged that at the
liturgical celebration she made a public declaration of
'faith in Hartcliffe'. In spite of its mounting problems of
vandalism, drug addiction, and unemployment, she would
go on living there.

   Jane's work in the Philippines includes the church's
ministry to children and young people, and she took
opportunities to listen to what children in England had to
say. She let them talk and become actively involved. She is
acutely aware of their vulnerability. Jesus is very demanding
when it comes to the care of children, she reminds us
(Matthew 18.1–10).

   On all four estates, people shared the stories of their
struggles together. Jane listened to the stories of young
mothers without partners, children growing up without
parents. She shared with them the problems of her own
people. She learnt that the poor in Britain had food and
benefits, but the mentally ill felt lost and lacked direction;
women refugees experienced no welcome and did not know
their rights. . . Some could not share their experiences. The
pain was too deep. In this context, the words of Jesus bring
hope and liberation: 'Take my yoke upon you, for my burden
is easy and my yoke is light.'

   'We are a damaged community,' commented one of the
Sisters. 'And we don't become whole without bearing the
pains of others.' As people opened up to one another, they
were encouraged to support one another and identify
actions they could take together to improve the quality
of their lives. This means 'listening to the Spirit', discussing

the problems: 'How can we move forward from where we are?' Here, Jane spoke of the 'NOW Testament'. 'What is God saying to us today?' she asked. 'Knowing the answer involves obedience. Hope is a gift, but is not given until we begin to move, act, and make a difference, somehow!'

And, on each of the estates, as they wove together the fabric of their experiences into a meaningful act of 'bonding', they learnt the whole process that culminated in a Christian celebration. In Ladywood, women expressed interest in the beautifully embroidered stoles and ribbons made by Filipino women to symbolize their struggle. Here, they said, we don't get together to do things. Later, in preparation for the celebration, an African girl taught them to make friendship bracelets and in 'the act of bonding' these were shared around as signs of mutual support and building community. In Bethnal Green, where there is a large community of Latin American and African refugees, the celebration drew much from the music and rhythms of their cultures. In one community, three generations of one family—grandmother, mother, and daughter—gave testimonies of faith. Children were encouraged to bring their contribution. In Bethnal Green, as they celebrated the Eucharist together, each person was asked to offer a brief prayer as he or she took the bread and wine. Jane prayed 'for the unshed tears of men— Jesus wept, so it is all right to cry—and for women who cry in joy and pain.' She helped everyone to integrate their experiences into worship, so that it was their liturgy, 'their offering as a people of God, to God'.

As a group of those who had set up the visit reflected together on the value of the project, they spoke of the strengthening of community awareness and the hope with which Jane inspired everyone—'a hope that cannot be bought'. The participants themselves were deeply moved that someone from outside had bothered to come. It helped, they said, to hear of the struggles of people like themselves in the Philippines, and to discover faith again and solidarity with them in suffering.

It was also a spiritual journey for Jane. 'My coming here is like a sparkler,' she said. 'God is already at work and has been at work all along. I simply blew away the dust so that your light can glow more brightly.' The focus of some of their discussion was the flame of a candle—'the flame of endurance and hope amid the darkness'. The light of bonfires is part of her culture. 'As fire burns, so negative feelings are breathed out: we dance and sing and pray; we relax and become receptive to new possibilities. We see hope together and somehow things are planned. When our connections begin to make sense, a personal conversion happens. Then it becomes a path towards social transformation, especially when we become deeply aware that "personal is political".'

Commitment to peace

SYDNEY and BRENDA BAILEY —

in New York and London

It was an Anglican bishop in 1930, proclaiming at a school speech day that the most honourable way to fulfil one's duty was to join the armed forces 'to defend and extend the British Empire', who set Sydney Bailey to take his first step in the direction of pacifism! The bishop, commenting on Jesus' words about 'rendering to Caesar . . .' made no reference to the following: '. . . and to God the things that are God's'. At fourteen years old, Sydney intuitively knew that the way of Jesus is the way of peace and became the only boy in the school to refuse to serve in the Officers' Training Corps.

From 1937, and as the Second World War became imminent, he started attending a Quaker meeting and later applied to join the Friends' Ambulance Unit, with whom he served as a conscientious objector for six years, both in East London and later in Burma and China. Pacifism is a vital part of Quaker witness. Friends refuse all weapons of violence and are well-known for their involvement in human rights, emergency aid, and other forms of humanitarian service.

For eight years, from 1946, Sydney Bailey worked with Commander Stephen King-Hall as editor of his weekly newsletter and then as Secretary of the Hansard Society for Parliamentary Government. King-Hall advocated 'defence without arms' as a policy for Britain. The object of war being 'to change the enemy's mind', he wanted the whole population to be trained in techniques of non-violent defence.

By 1954, Sydney Bailey, beginning to question whether it was enough to refuse to take up arms, came to see that the pacifist must help to remove the causes of war and build peace in a positive way: 'If we say "No" to all war, we have an obligation to do our utmost to prevent it from ever happening.' Sydney and his wife Brenda offered to work at Quaker House in New York, an integral part of the Quaker presence at the United Nations. Friends have been active at the UN since its founding Conference at San Francisco in 1945 and before that in the League of Nations. Through Quaker influence, at the beginning of the first session of the General Assembly and at the end of the last session, one minute's silence is set aside for prayer or meditation. Friends were also instrumental in providing a meditation room, with a non-sectarian atmosphere, in the UN building. Their main role at the UN is to protect and strengthen spiritual and moral perspectives in peace-building, to be 'pastors' to ministers and diplomats, entering with sympathy into their painful dilemmas and the difficult choices they have to make.

At the UN, Sydney worked with problems like disarma-

ment and whether the procedures of the Security Council
could be organized in a more effective way. He sought to
transform the 'right of veto' into the more positive 'way of
seeking unanimity'.

From 1958 to 1960, Sydney Bailey was Visiting Research
Scholar at the Carnegie Endowment for International Peace.
At the UN and since 1960, he worked as a political mediator,
organizing conferences for diplomats, serving on a number
of Foreign Office and ecumenical committees alongside his
considerable research and writing. He has written fifteen
books on the United Nations, disarmament, and human
rights. Some have been published in French, Portuguese,
Arabic, Hindi, and Japanese. His skill and commitment to
peace are internationally recognized.

The most challenging part of his work has been his
involvement in political mediation, particularly in the
Middle East and Northern Ireland. Quakers worldwide are
often called in where a third party is needed to settle a
dispute, and may even propose the terms of settlement.

One example was in 1973. Sydney Bailey had been
approached in December 1972 by an Egyptian friend with
proposals for direct talks between Egypt and Israel for a
bilateral peace settlement. After long and careful consid-
eration as to whether such a mission might be harmful to
Israel's Arab neighbours and Palestine, he and an American
Quaker, Paul Johnson, went to Israel for informal talks with
friends in the Foreign Ministry, putting before them the
Egyptian suggestion and their Quaker principles:

> . . . direct talks between the two sides without pre-
> conditions, a moratorium on such future public statements
> by either party as might make a settlement more difficult
> to achieve, and an understanding by both parties that
> positions previously adopted should not be barriers to the
> possibility of agreements of substance.

(This and subsequent indented quotations are from Sydney
Bailey's 1993 Swarthmore Lecture, 'Peace is a Process'
[Quaker Home Service and Woodbrooke College].)

Helped by the Bishop of London and the Anglican Archbishop in Jerusalem to get the message to a senior Israeli, they received a positive response and met at the YMCA in East Jerusalem on 28 January 1973. Their reception at the Foreign Ministry the next day seemed cold and unco-operative, but gradually discussion opened up and it was agreed that the two Quakers and one of the Israelis would prepare a written account of the Egyptian proposals and a summary of their discussion that day. Five days later they met again, but with a warmer welcome. They were informed that the message from the Quakers had been considered 'at the highest level of the Israeli government', and that Israel was ready for talks with Egypt but needed the assurance that the Egyptians were acting on the full authority of President Sadat. The discussions which followed were procrastinating and inconclusive. Direct talks with Egypt were not possible at this stage and only five Israelis knew anything about the meeting. Discussions continued in the Middle East and London. Sydney and Brenda Bailey entertained Egyptian and Israeli officials in their home in London but never simultaneously. It was not until 1978, long after the Arab-Israeli War (4 October 1973) that Egypt and Israel met at Camp David and the bilateral peace treaty was signed in 1979. It was not easy to evaluate the results of their initial mediation and to know whether it was the right use of limited resources. A pamphlet published ten years later by Mordechai Gazit, head of Golda Meir's office, suggested a 'fundamental change' of policy less than a month after their visit. But other authorities suggested that the concession rested later on Kissinger.

Quaker mediation does not expect to see quick results but to build bridges of trust, setting goals that may not be achieved in the lifetime of the mediator. The primary task of mediators is to help both sides to begin to communicate. Well-informed of each situation before they enter it, they are good listeners, seeking to offer the only opportunity some leaders have to articulate the pain of long-standing intractable problems. Mediators do not know all the answers and are often very vulnerable. They are not always given adequate information, or they may be given false information, but working in small groups of two or three they know the strength of team work. An incident like that in which Sydney Bailey took part in Jerusalem is an integral part of a worldwide network of Quaker activity, facilitated by previous humanitarian relief work on both sides of conflicts and by maintaining contacts over many years. The final result is never due to the work of one person or to one event. Quaker mediators are known at both national and international levels for their advocacy, both in writing and speaking out on issues like human rights, refugees, and disarmament. Being entirely neutral, they have no political power and work only to reconcile 'people to people'. Sydney Bailey likes to deal with officials 'face to face', 'for I do not find it easy to answer that of God in the other person on the phone or by post.'

Conferences for diplomats and their families—private off-the-record conferences—have contributed much to the bridge-building process. Their overall theme is important: national interest and international responsibility. Participants, who play a key role in relieving international tension and who include some who may go on to higher office, come not to speak for their governments, but to listen and learn from one another. The media are not present and no written reports are expected. As well as time for discussion on issues and research of current concern, time is set aside for social activities. These are often the most effective means of dissolving personal misgivings between political opponents. Sydney Bailey tells, for example, of a diplomat from a Second World War occupied country who was drawn to play as tennis partner with a diplomat from an Axis country and they won. Friendship began to develop when they discovered they had been in the same region at the end of the war and had shared common experiences of cold, hunger, loneliness and fear. In a conference in the 1970s an Arab diplomat, who was unwilling to have anything to do with Israelis and boycotted discussion groups, found that his two children were playing football with the children of the Israeli diplomat. And then at the closing party, he invited the beautiful daughter of the Israeli diplomat to dance with him.

Quaker peacemakers and mediators are respected for their 'transparent honesty' and impartiality. They are friends of leaders on both sides of a conflict. Their motive is love: love of God and one's neighbour, an impartial love which does not take sides. Every genuine Quaker concern for peace, Sydney Bailey says, comes from God: 'to build a world in which outward weapons are not needed to ensure justice'. Bringing outer peace, Sydney Bailey says, depends on inner peace and love within:

> Pacifism is not passivism: it is a fruit of love, a source of encouragement in the face of disappointment, of tranquillity in situations of turmoil, of patience in periods of tedium, of courage in times of danger.

Sydney's wife Brenda, who has shared his commitment to peace and supported him in everything, developed her own role in building community. Coming from a German Quaker family who offered protection to many Jews in Germany, she trained as a social worker and registered as a 'conscientious objector' in the Second World War. She met Sydney while working with the Friends' Ambulance Unit in East London and they were married in 1945. During their time in New York, they lived close to the UN building and she was able to attend meetings. Africa became her major interest and it was exciting for her to be present in the process of decolonization. It was good for them as a family to be fully involved in the conferences for diplomats. They met so many people from all over the world, formed many lasting friendships, and their understanding of people was profoundly enriched.

In New York, Brenda worked part-time with the American Friends Committee, running a clothing centre for Algerian refugees, shipped clothing to Algeria and later, back in Britain, became chairperson of the Quaker Algerian

Committee. After the Notting Hill riots, concerned about race relations in Britain, she pursued her interest in community organization and started training in community development. She persuaded the Quaker Race Relations Committee to open the Neighbourhood House in Islington to provide a home for an African family on the top floor, and to use the ground floor for a multiracial preschool playgroup and housing advice centre. Her children were by now in secondary school and she had time to become involved on a number of Community Relations Councils and in marriage guidance counselling. This became a very interesting period for her. She co-ordinated a group working together to create a new building set in a small park for the Caxton House Settlement at Archway. This was to serve all age groups in a multiracial housing development. When this project was completed in 1975, Quaker Peace and Service asked her to continue to raise money for their overseas projects and this involved many journeys to rural areas in Africa and the Middle East.

Both Sydney and Brenda Bailey have experienced the truth that all communities are equal in the sight of God. At his level, Sydney was given opportunities to meet with heads of governments and liberation movements. 'But mediation is not only the work of specialists,' he says. 'It is the task of all.' Although Brenda travelled with him on most of his peace missions, her activities symbolize peacemaking in the local community to which all of us are called. At the heart of all peacemaking is a skill that few seem to have, although it is possible for each one of us to cultivate it: the skill of good listening. Those engaged in conflict, whether at an international, local, or personal level complain that others fail to understand their grievances.

> The follower of Jesus is to discover and then promote the Kingdom of God. That Kingdom has two tenses: it is already here, in each one of us; and it is still to come, when God's goodness becomes a universal norm. We are to live now 'as if' the Kingdom of God were already fulfilled.

Peace begins within ourselves. It is to be implemented within the family, in our Meetings, in our work and leisure, in our own localities, and internationally. The task will never be done. Peace is a process to engage in, not a goal to be reached.

A dialogue with Africa

AYLWARD SHORTER –
Britain to East and Central Africa

Aylward Shorter's father, an Egyptologist at the British Museum, kindled within him a deep fascination to explore the many cultures of Africa. Although his father died at the age of thirty-two—leaving his mother, a remarkable person and a devout Catholic, with four children to bring up at the end of World War 2—his influence remained an integral part of their family life. From the earliest days he can remember, Aylward thought of his future in the Roman Catholic priesthood. His education in two Benedictine schools with their tradition of fine Catholic liturgy satisfied an intuitive need for the aesthetic in worship. 'The worship was so beautiful, it made you want to pray,' he said.

At eighteen, the rude reality of basic training in National Service came as a real culture shock after the sheltered atmosphere of Downside School and he resolved he would return and ask to join the monastery. Then a letter from a school friend in Zimbabwe saying, 'Come to Africa' re-kindled his earlier interest and in 1951 he was seconded to the Third Kenya Battalion in Nanyuki. Although he was permitted little social contact with African soldiers in colonial Kenya, he learnt to speak Swahili and discovered the thrill of being able to communicate with people whose culture was different from his own. Most of the 700 Kenyans in his battalion were Christians and he became aware of their natural religious feelings.

After about four to six weeks, he was sent to Khota Tingi in Malaya, to train Kenyans in the art of jungle warfare. If nothing else, he learnt a lot about Africa from homesick askaris (East African soldiers or policemen). Several were wounded and some died. There were moments of conversion to faith. Again, he was struck by their religious attitude and grew close to them in their prayers.

In 1952, Aylward went up to Oxford University to study modern history, realizing that he was not called to be a Benedictine monk but to return to East Africa. He made contact with the White Fathers (now known as 'Missionaries of Africa') and was encouraged to complete his degree. This was followed by two years studying philosophy in Ireland, attending a noviciate in Holland and a multicultural study experience at a theological seminary in Ottawa—a time of spiritual growth and changing attitudes. In 1961 a mystical experience at Pentecost confirmed his oath 'to serve Africa for life' and he returned to Britain to prepare to enter the priesthood. After ordination in 1962 he was sent to Rome for African studies. This brought him under the influence of Joseph Goetz, an anthropologist who encouraged him to return to Oxford to read for a postgraduate diploma and doctorate in anthropology. In 1964, for the most important part of his research, he went to live among the Kimbu, in a remote rural area of Tanzania. At a more profound level than in the army, he learnt from the people's religious experience. By gaining a thorough knowledge of their language, he set about analysing myths, proverbs, folk-tales, praise-names, songs, rituals, and regalia to discover their basic religious concepts.

The Kimbu, a Bantu-speaking group who live in densely wooded country bounded by rivers, are hunter-gatherers, cultivating maize and collecting honey. Their two centres of interest are the forest, the home of malevolent spirits, and the village which includes the spirits of departed ancestors. As in some other parts of East Africa, the Sun, *Ilyuva*, is the Supreme Being (not to be simply identified with *ilyunsi*, meaning 'sun' or 'sunlight'). As the sun gives life and destroys it, so *Ilyuva* gives life and punishes evil deeds. When making oaths and calling upon the Supreme Being to witness to the truth, he heard them say '*Ilyuva* has seen it.' Although they rarely prayed directly to God but to their ancestors, whom they believed were in the arms of God, they concluded with the same words, '*Ilyuva* has seen it.' Another name for the Supreme Being is *Matunda* (from an ancient word meaning 'to mould pottery') meaning 'creator'. These are just a few examples of the rich symbolism which bridges the sacred and secular in all African religions—a welcome relief from the cold rationalization of western philosophy. When you take symbolism away, he says, there is nothing left to help us see the spiritual.

Living with rural people Aylward saw how the world of nature impinges on the human world and becomes a bridge to the world of the spirits. In traditional folk-tales animals talk and express human values. Graphic descriptions, imitations of sounds and a profound reverence for all life, animate and inanimate, make storytelling an art in which African peoples excel. Poetry too is shared. He met many who could bring a poetic imagination and a gift of words to the life of the community. And, he reflected, living in the village week after week, meeting the same people, sharing their everyday concerns and times of celebration was not unlike life in a Benedictine monastery! There was the same need 'to create one's own space, to stand back with respect, and build up the humanity of others'. He learnt that technology is not the most important aspect of human development. Kimbu village elders might be technologically ignorant but were men of profound dignity and wisdom. Aylward Shorter stayed with the Kimbu for two years as priest and friend until 1967 when he returned to Oxford to write his thesis.

From 1968, he served as a founder member with the Pastoral Institute of East Africa at Gaba near Kampala,

Uganda, for the next nine years. This work put him in touch
with the whole of Africa. Among his students were men
and women who held important posts in the dioceses of
countries in East and Central Africa and some from
West and Southern Africa. His responsibilities took him to
consultations in many parts of the continent and, as an
'agent of renewal', he warmed to the challenge of apply-
ing the insights of Vatican 2.

From 1971, Aylward Shorter taught for a brief time in
Eldoret in Kenya, Kipalapala in Tanzania, the University of
Bristol, in Kenya again and since 1988, as principal of a
missionary college in London. He has written many books
and made a significant contribution to the development of
African theology. He continues to visit Kenya frequently and
keeps in touch with many of his former students. These have
been enriching relationships, a vital part of his 'ongoing
dialogue with Africa'. In his present appointment, one of his
chief concerns is to encourage cross-cultural exchanges and
enable students to learn, as he did, through real encounters.

Unlike most colonialists who made little effort to understand Africans except from the standpoint of their own
culture, Aylward Shorter believes that a real exchange of
insights and growth of mutual understanding are possible.
His basic conviction is that African Christian theology must
grow out of a *dialogue* between Christianity and indigenous
religions—a process that he calls 'inculturation'. There is no
room here for paternalism. African traditional religions are
not to be regarded as of mere antiquarian interest but to
be respected as living traditions, while recognizing their
plurality. 'Pluralism is not a mere diversity, but diversity-in-
unity,' he says in one of his books, *African Christian Theology*
(Orbis 1991). It has a richness 'patterned on the organic
unity of the Trinity itself.' The Kimbu are just one example
of hundreds more tribal groups. Every community has its
own distinctive traditions, values, beliefs, imagery, and cere-
monies. Although there are few common factors, all African
religions are rich in symbolism and this is mostly expressed
in non-verbal ways, through dance, drama, and ritual.

Dialogue, which takes account of all factors, begins through living encounters with Africans at grassroots level as Christians and traditional Africans become aware of what they can learn from one another. Africans on their side 'should not abandon western ideas and methods. These are channels of communication which must not be blocked.'

Aylward Shorter believes that dialogue leads to a mutual respect which rejoices not only in areas where we agree, but in our essential differences. It acknowledges elements in African religions that are superior to current Christian insights 'that could reawaken or draw out dormant and latent themes in the Christian tradition'. Africa has much to teach the world. 'Dialogue between Christianity and African traditional religions is without doubt part of God's plan,' he says.

Africa does not separate spiritual and secular experiences, but integrates them into the whole of life. British Christians need to be convinced, not only that there is much to learn from Africa, but to see their own local church as the place where dialogue between faith and culture must happen, to look at the theology behind it and discover God's word which is 'incarnate' in every time and place.

Learning from people of other faiths

IVY GUTRIDGE – in Wolverhampton

'Ivy, I don't understand you. We used to send missionaries "out there", but now "they" are over here and you are making friends with them!' said one of Ivy's friends some years ago. For many years, Ivy Gutridge has worked with people of other faiths without going outside her town. Until 1975, when

she was asked to become Secretary of the Wolverhampton
Inter-Faith Group, she had been what she describes as a
'church Christian': her life revolved around church, Sunday
school, and family. Recollecting the prayer she had repeated
many times from the Methodist Covenant service—'Put me
to what you will. . .'— she accepted the challenge. Previously
she had scarcely noticed the presence of Hindus, Jews,
Muslims, Sikhs, and even other Christian denominations
living round her, but all these and their places of worship
suddenly became significant and her life opened up in many
unexpected ways.

At that time, there were only thirty members in the Inter-
Faith Group in Wolverhampton (WIFG). She made up her
mind to deliver the mailings, knock on their doors, and get
to know them. Most invited her in and began to talk to her
about their faith and asked Ivy about hers. Just by sitting
and listening, she learnt so much from their spirituality and
particularly from their devotion to prayer. Sometimes when
phoning a Muslim or Hindu family, their response would
be, 'Sorry, we're at prayer at the moment. Can we talk later
please.' That had never happened when ringing a Christian
home, she reflected.

Inter-Faith meetings, where individuals shared what their
faith meant to them, challenged her to start digging deeper
into what she believed. She had always been a contented
Christian, who asked few questions and had not needed to
articulate her beliefs. Now she needed to know more about
her faith and read the Bible more carefully to give a clearer
account of what she believed.

Her first visit to another place of worship was to a Guru
Ravidass temple where she was invited to share in the women's
afternoon and listen to their hymns, sung in Punjabi to the
accompaniment of Indian music and rhythms. It was an
unforgettable experience: the colour, the sounds, their devotion, and reverence. It was strange, bewildering, and deeply
moving. Although the women knew little English and she
didn't know their language, she felt a warmth of welcome
and love coming out to meet her. They invited her to teach

them English and, over the next five years, while she also attempted to learn to speak Punjabi, she formed many strong friendships.

'Why do you come?' they asked.

'Because I am a Christian and Jesus taught us to love our neighbours,' she replied.

One very old lady at the temple put her arms round her one afternoon, saying in Punjabi, 'This is real love.'

There were many invitations to the homes of her new friends. Their hospitality was overwhelming. She wrote, 'The strange but beautiful experience of being invited to Asian and Caribbean homes helped to convince me that in spite of my fears I was being led in answer to prayer.'

Ivy had never expected to become a public speaker, but, when others wanted to hear what she was doing, she found herself responding to numerous invitations to speak in public of her experiences and, although she had not trained as a lay preacher, these invitations sometimes included preaching and leading worship. This too challenged her to look more deeply into her Scriptures.

It was a period of searching and growth. There were many hard questions, like those put to her by fellow Christians. Some accused her of betraying Christ by going into temples. At one meeting someone said, 'If what you say is true, my whole life has been a sham!' and walked out and slammed the door. Others thanked her for making them think. Another handed her a beautifully decorated card with the words, 'It is good to be sincere but you might be sincerely wrong.' It was a painful experience, but looking back, she said she was grateful for it and for the challenge it made to her loyalty to Christ. There were times when, if it hadn't been for her 'covenant with God', Ivy would have given up. Sitting on the temple floor with women while they worshipped, she asked herself, 'Am I being disloyal? Should I be here?' She prayed earnestly for guidance. Some words from the book of Samuel—'God looks upon the heart'—came to her. Believing that God had led her this far, she prayed that God would continue to direct her.

Ivy learnt far more about her own faith than she realized was possible and discovered much about the experience of God from others, particularly in prayer. She was able to move sometimes from being an observer and questioner to the experience of being lifted up to God in silent prayer and meditation, especially through the haunting melodies and rhythms of Hindu religious music.

She reached the stage where she could do no other but acknowledge their deep spirituality and the validity of their faith. At first, she had hesitated when Sikhs bowed to the Guru Granth, their holy book. She stood and bowed towards the congregation to symbolize her greeting to them. Now that she is more familiar with the riches of their Scriptures, she can bow in respect, though she does not go down to the ground with her friends in complete devotion. 'I could not bring myself to believe that God did not hear and accept their prayers and worship,' she said. There were Sikhs, Ravidassis, Hindus, Muslims, and Buddhists whose beliefs affected their whole lives and who, when her husband died in 1983, came as close as her Christian friends in sharing her sorrow. Her church was packed with people of many faiths for his funeral. Prayers were said and tributes expressed by Muslim, Sikh, and Hindu representatives, a spontaneous mark of deep respect and affection 'to our brother Ken'. The funeral became a 'celebration of our varied beliefs about life after death'.

Although she is modest about her achievements, it is very largely through Ivy's persistence and availability that the Wolverhampton Inter-Faith Group has become one of the most successful in the country. In 1982, the group became a registered charity and opened up an Inter-Faith Office and Resource Centre. Members' involvement has increased in latter years. Small groups have been formed to discuss the theological, cultural, and practical aspects of health, immigration, police liaison, women's and young people's concerns. WIFG is recognized as a consultancy for matters of reconciliation and service in the community. The group is represented on the Community Health Council Ethnic

Minorities Committee, on the Race Equality Council and in other groups which monitor community needs. They are called in as mediators in political–religious disputes such as the occasion when a primary school Sikh boy was forbidden to wear his turban to school. On that occasion, discussions with the police, community and religious leaders, the family, and press 'added up to many hours of peacemaking'. The more Ivy became involved, the more her conviction grew that she was sharing in God's work of reconciliation.

Many others in Wolverhampton have been encouraged to start the journey Ivy has taken. For example, a local vicar wrote of evensong being cancelled in the parish church while his elderly congregation accepted an invitation to join the Diwali celebration at the local Hindu temple. For many, whose grandchildren have Hindu friends at school, it was their first experience of non-Christian worship and they were overwhelmed by the welcome and hospitality.

In January each year, WIFG arranges for all faiths to come together to pray for peace. Members pray in their own language; translations are provided. It may not be possible for people of different faiths to pray together, but silent prayer and meditation is helpful to many believers. At one of the first of such occasions, the climax came when a child lit a candle of peace from which others took their light. The increasing light this created symbolized their growing acceptance, understanding, and commitment to carry the light of peace into the world. These services have become very meaningful to Ivy.

Despite her lack of academic qualifications, Ivy has had invitations to speak to a wide range of professionals about working with people of other faiths: college professors, nursery nurses, teachers, police, and social workers. In 1976, with the help of a professional photographer and a student, she put together a photographic exhibition on 'Ways of worship in Wolverhampton', which was displayed in the art gallery for a month. School teachers responded immediately, asking for contact people in the various communities. Three text books were prepared using some of the photographs, and a slide and tape sequence that Ivy put together has been used by hundreds of people. The Inter-Faith Network links over sixty groups in Britain. Ivy was on the steering committee and was elected one of its vice-chairpersons in 1993.

Back in 1984, she was asked to represent the World Congress of Faiths at the World Conference on Religion and Peace (WCRP) in Nairobi. She met so many people who had hope in God and cared for peace; it was an unforgettable experience. Since then, she has attended other conferences in Australia, Northern Italy, and Vienna and been invited to write reports for them. WCRP now operates across all five continents. It does not try to draw people from one faith to another but, with respect and tolerance, seeks to create the security that is the harbinger of peace. These conferences have been experiences of mutual discovery, learning from one another's Scriptures and building bridges of understanding by sharing concern for issues of peace, justice, and the environment. All religions encourage believers to work for peace.

Ivy is continually increasing her awareness of where beliefs are similar and where they differ. 'We rejoice when we agree together, but are open and honest about where we do not agree.' On one of many occasions, when the Group held a 'Faith Tour', over 200 people experienced first the exuberance of singing in the Salvation Army citadel and the 'alleluias' and handclapping at a black Caribbean church. Then they went on to experience the devout discipline of prayer at a mosque, the colourful scene of the Sikh gurdwara, an exotic, noisy celebration of a Hindu festival and finally came to the Quaker meeting house where they sat for ten minutes in prayerful silence. In each place, they saw that God is worshipped in sincerity and truth. And by demonstrating their oneness, they believed they were presenting an effective example of multifaith harmony and that people of no faith are more likely to discover faith when they see believers of different religious traditions working together in unity for the peace of the world.

Building trust

ELIZABETH HARRIS –
Britain to Sri Lanka

One *Poya* Day (full moon), in Sri Lanka, Elizabeth Harris found herself speaking to a group of Buddhist women, sharing with them her reflections on Buddhist texts that meant a lot to her: texts about meditation, social justice, and values that both Buddhists and Christians hold in common. It was strange to be sitting there as a Christian speaking to them about their faith! She was deeply moved by the trust expressed in their invitation.

Having qualified as a teacher in 1973, Elizabeth taught English for two years in Jamaica—her first experience of living in another culture and a very formative one. During the next four years she taught in London, until her longing to be involved in something more world-oriented again led her to work for Christians Abroad, the organization which had helped to organize her contract in Jamaica. As Inform-ation Secretary in their London office she was often involved in interviews and discussions with people going to work in other parts of the world. What challenged her most was being able to prepare them to enter another culture to listen and receive.

In 1984, Elizabeth visited Sri Lanka with an all-age team sent by Christians Aware and began to develop a deep interest and empathy for Sri Lanka and Buddhism. The following year, she heard of an invitation from the Ecumenical Institute for Study and Dialogue in Colombo for people to come and study issues of religion, justice, and peace in Sri Lanka. Convinced that Christians should cross cultural and religious boundaries and learn from other faiths, she applied for a scholarship from the World Council of

Churches. Buddhism attracted her because of its emphasis
on non-violence and meditation. But she did not want to
study 'comparative religion' or to be primarily involved in
dialogue. Neither approach seemed adequate. She wanted
to 'enter' Buddhism and experience it—what Kenneth
Cracknell (in his book *Towards a New Relationship*) describes
as 'a passing over into another religion and coming back'. It
involved a new religious encounter—letting go of all that had
conditioned her and accepting the risk of having to cope
with the terrible vacuum that might be left. Pure academic
study would have been much easier. But she believed that
such an experience would enable her to come back and see
Christianity in a new way.

That year, she studied for a diploma in Buddhism at
the Postgraduate Institute for Pali and Buddhist Studies
(affiliated to the University of Kelaniya). This gave her a
basic introduction to Buddhism and its philosophy. But
alongside this, she began to form close friendships with
Buddhists, to visit their temples, to learn from them and
practise meditation, to visit inter-faith groups and become
involved in development, justice, and peace issues.

At the end of the year, Elizabeth decided to attempt an
MA in Buddhism, and continued to deepen her friendship
with Buddhist people of faith. Aloysius Pieris, an internationally renowned theologian and Indologist—who had
himself studied Buddhism under the guidance of a Buddhist
monk, and who had been her spiritual guide into Buddhism
—invited her to become his research assistant at Tulana
near Colombo. Tulana is a place where Christians and
Buddhists meet for study and meditation. It has some interesting works of religious art painted by a Buddhist monk,
including one of Jesus washing the feet of disciples who
wear the saffron robes of the *Sangha* (order of monks). At
first the work was rather tedious, sorting out the library and
cataloguing books, until Father Aloysius began to encourage
her to attempt a major piece of research into the encounter
between Buddhism and Britain in the nineteenth century—
what the British wrote about Buddhism—a topic very

relevant to contemporary Buddhist–Christian relationships. In 1993 she completed her thesis for a doctorate. For those four years she was supported financially by a number of trusts, some of which have a particular interest in inter-religious encounter, like the Max Warren Fellowship and Spalding Trust.

Elizabeth's journey into Sri Lanka led her both into the pain of a country divided by violence and into the struggles and hopes of truly religious people. One of the pilgrimages she joined was to Sri Pada (Mountain of the Holy Footprint), in the centre of the island. It was an amazing experience climbing through the night, with other pilgrims, some quite elderly, to 13,000 feet above sea level. At the summit, each pilgrim rang a bell the number of times he or she had been there. Some had been twenty or thirty times. The atmosphere was one of true devotion, symbolizing so much of Elizabeth's seven years' experience. She had lived among a people of real faith, full of love and compassion, and full of a spiritual sense; they had taught her to think more deeply about prayer and to value silence. 'And so I was forced to ask the question', she says, 'Is this blessed by God? If I believe in a God of love, I must believe it is blessed. For wherever there is compassion and spiritual awareness, there is God.' And in all the time she spent with them in their temples, in meditation, listening to the chant of the *Pirit*, passing flowers along the line, lighting candles, she did not feel she was betraying her Christian faith, but showing reverence for a great teacher and experiencing bonds of love with Buddhists there.

This devotional Buddhism, which is rooted in the Buddhist texts, is nurtured through meditation and expresses itself in a very profound reverence for the Buddha, in doing good, gaining merit for one's relations and oneself, and progressing towards a better rebirth. Elizabeth learnt much from the people and their religious texts. She discovered that the Buddha was a teacher she could respect: a likeable, human, practical, down-to-earth teacher of infinite compassion, 'someone who stressed the need for right action rather than

ritual and dogma'. Although many students of Buddhism
link its teachings with the mystical, Elizabeth saw in Buddhism
a teacher who encouraged people not to think about eternal
questions—like: How did the world begin? How will it end?
What happens after death?— but who said, 'What is important is how you live now.' He spoke of the destruction of
selfishness and the responsibility of the state, king, and
government to create economic justice, peace, and harmony
for all; a side of Buddhism which some groups in Sri Lanka
are trying to recover.

One of Elizabeth's main interests in coming to Sri Lanka
was to learn from Buddhist meditation. First, she discovered
that the western stereotype of Buddhists spending regular,
long hours in meditation is not quite true, though they do
have a rich experience from which we can learn, especially
mettā, meditation. Elizabeth explained in an article in the
Ceylon Churchman, 'At its heart is the directing of loving kind-
ness to all people. *Mettā* is one of the four qualities central to
the Buddhist life, together with *karunā*—compassion, *muditā*
—the ability to feel joy at another's success—and *upekkhā*—
equanimity. In one meditation session attended, we were
encouraged to imagine *mettā* as a stream of light which we
were to allow to flow to our neighbours, our relations, those
whom we disliked and to all beings in the world. It is a
practice which brings peace and tranquillity. Preoccupation
with self flows away.'

In all her friendships with Buddhists, Elizabeth learnt what
their faith means to them, and emphasized to them those
elements we share—being open to the needs of the poor, the
compassion of Christ and the Buddha, and other aspects of
spiritual awareness. Christians tend to say that when a person
has accepted Christ, everything is put right. But is the human
personality purified automatically? Elizabeth began to learn
that Buddhist meditation in the Theravada tradition was
essentially a form of mind-training: that through it she could
see how her mind worked and how craving and other negative emotions could be recognized and dealt with before
they damage the whole personality. One of the monks who

taught her said, 'Suffering, pain, and feelings of anger are not suppressed but faced, confronted, and transformed.'

One western stereotype of Buddhism is that Buddhist detachment is indifference. Elizabeth was made more aware of this and became more determined to challenge it when she heard a Christian say, 'I would rather see the robes of Christ stained with dust than the Buddha smiling above the suffering of the world.' She learnt that detachment is not indifference, for the detachment Buddha teaches is de-attachment from lust and possessiveness, from *rāga*, the greed that destroys society and world peace. Detachment is *virāga*, without lust, and fosters the discernment which can see injustice objectively. She points out that central to Buddhism is the analysis of cause, and that the texts stress that the wise must speak out about what is right and wrong. She is adamant that nothing in Buddhism encourages indifference to suffering but rather that everything stresses the importance of compassion. She says that her experience has certainly been that Buddhists have a deep concern for people, their rights to land, and their rights as human beings.

Elizabeth stresses that 'entering' another religion does not mean putting critical faculties aside. Through her knowledge of Buddhist texts, she found that she was critical of some aspects of modern Buddhist belief and that she could challenge some of them. In 1987, for example, when a huge bomb exploded at a main bus station in Colombo, some of her friends said that those who died must have done something evil in their past. Their bad *karma* had resulted in their being there at that time. From her knowledge of the texts, she could remind them of the Buddha's words that not all present happenings can be explained by past actions. Other elements enter. There are seven possible reasons, only one of which is *karma*. And Elizabeth's answer was confirmed by a monk, to whom the question was also referred.

Among some of the Buddhist middle-class, she was aware of a territorial exclusivism that has nothing to do with the core of Buddhism. Violent ethnic war between mainly

Hindu Tamils and Buddhist Sinhalese forced her to ask of Sri Lankans: How is there civil war in a religious country? Part of the problem is that Sri Lankan Buddhists have a 'Holy Land' tradition, rather like the Jews in Israel. They believe that Buddha blessed them and gave Sri Lanka to become the place where Buddhism would flourish. But this myth works against the pluralist reality. Although religion is not the only factor in the ethnic conflict, Sri Lanka is a country where four religions meet and until this challenge is faced and accepted at gut level, there will not be peace. Elizabeth has supported several peace initiatives which bring together Christians, Buddhists, Hindus, and Muslims.

Her experience has also confirmed that it is not possible to iron out all the differences and find a common core. Christians and Buddhists have different starting points which need to be mutually acknowledged and respected. Buddhists deny the idea of a creator God and a personal saviour. The Buddha is the supreme symbol of what is good and holy and the texts are full of wonderful sayings about *Nirvana*, the highest and most ineffable bliss. She learnt that the 'touching points' between the two religions centre on humanity rather than divinity. 'Gods' in Buddhism are on a level with 'saints' in Christianity. They can help but are lesser beings than the Buddhas. But here lies a challenge which Christians tend to ignore—to work out how to relate to a religion that is so different and to learn from it and be enriched by it.

Elizabeth maintains that it is arrogance for Christians to believe that only they have *the* truth. This attitude denies that God is at work in all the world. All religions are unique. Christianity cannot claim to be the only religion in which God is working to bring harmony to the world, nor should Christians challenge people to leave their faith. Buddhism is a totally fulfilling religion and does not need Christianity to complement or fulfil it. The history of mission in Asia confirms this. Only about seven per cent of Sri Lankans and three per cent of Indians have become Christians compared to over fifty per cent in many parts of Africa.

A missionary in 1894 likened Buddhism to 'a dead corpse'

and added, 'it cannot be revived but with the spirit of the devil'! As a consequence of this and similar comments stretching right across the century, the mistrust of Christians which developed in the Buddhist mind has never been eradicated. Elizabeth's research has shown that it was the exclusivism of British Christian missionaries that led to the Buddhist revival of the late nineteenth century. This approach discredited Christianity, communicating a false image of God as one who divides people according to whether they 'believe' or not.

In her final year, Elizabeth was asked to invite some Buddhist women to speak about what Buddhism said about violence to a conference of the Women's Commission of the National Christian Council. She had considerable difficulty in persuading them. Two friends eventually agreed but only came because Elizabeth would be with them. Later, they told her that they had been warned not to accept because the Christians 'would want to use them'. Elizabeth too was hesitant, having been at meetings where Buddhist speakers had felt their religion was being threatened. In fact, the meeting went really well. Christians who came were very moved by the spirituality and conviction of the Buddhist women. Some searching questions were asked in a spirit of love. Her friends returned home encouraged.

What then is the missionary role in Sri Lanka in the Decade of Evangelism? Elizabeth's seven years of learning from the people and texts of Buddhism was in itself a mission—being a bridge between people who know little of one another, building trust and understanding. Elizabeth believes that missionaries who will do this and share the wonderful example Christ brings are desperately needed in Sri Lanka—missionaries who will question the real evils of selfishness, racism, and the imbalance of trade relationships. And they will demonstrate that God, who is full of infinite love and compassion, has blessed the whole human race.

3

Some biblical perspectives

These twenty stories are each a different response to the call of Christ, illustrating the variety of gifts the Spirit gives for mission. They cover many issues, challenges, questions, and dilemmas. In a changing world, there are no ready-made answers, but the Spirit goes on bombarding us with new insights and new ways of mission, and extends our boundaries beyond our imagining. The following Bible studies are offered as a way to explore some of the issues. They can be used purely for personal study and reflection or by groups. At the end of each, suggestions for leaders of house groups are printed in italics.

i Welcome

Read **Luke 7.36–50**, trying to identify with

● **the Pharisee**, an upholder of the *status quo*. According to tradition, he thanked God daily that he was a man and not a woman, a Jew and not a Gentile. The title Pharisee meant 'separate'. His strict adherence to the Law kept him apart from immoral people and from befriending many who might have needed help. The fact that he invited Jesus to a meal may suggest a glimmer of interest in Jesus, but he brought to the encounter a heavy load of preconceptions and conservatism. It was not only his neglect of the usual courtesies which made Jesus feel unwelcome, but his inability to 'hear' what Jesus had to say.
● **the woman**, maybe a prostitute, recognizing her emptiness, that poverty of spirit which Jesus called 'blessed' (Matthew 5.3), welcomed the gift of reconciliation to God

in a way that Simon would never be capable of doing, unless he too repented.

Now look at **Matthew 10.5–14** and **40–42**, where Jesus lays down some principles for our involvement in mission:

- Mission begins where we are, in the community where God has placed us (verses 5 and 6).
- Mission is holistic. It reaches everyone, and brings healing of mind and body, restoring to those who have been stigmatized the respect that is due to them as children of God (verse 8).
- We are to make ourselves vulnerable, unprotected by wealth and possessions but dependent upon those with whom we work, so that nothing stands in the way of our partnership in building the Kingdom (verses 9 and 10).
- This leads us to identify those who support us. The Kingdom grows where there is mutual support and acceptance (verse 11).
- We are to be sensitive to areas where we are unwelcome. If there is no welcome, God's mission through us will have no more effect than it had on Simon the Pharisee. Notice the frequent use of the word 'welcome' (GNB and NJB) and 'receive' (NIV and REB) in verses 12–14 and 40–42. How do these verses relate to Luke 7.44–46?

Real welcome to those through whom God is working is crucial in both church and society:

- Can you recall times when you or your local church may have forced your presence or stayed in areas where you were not welcome? Reflect on this in relation to Stephen Barton's feelings on page 3 and to Elizabeth Harris's findings on pages 120–1.
- Make a list of occasions when Jesus was unwelcome. How did he respond in each case?
- Reflect on the way the Spirit led Paul through Asia Minor in Acts 16.6-8. What can we learn from his experience in this Decade of Evangelism?

● Look again at Matthew 10.40–42 and reflect on their meaning, especially in relation to Christians who come to us from other parts of the world, like Margaret Conteh (pages 25–6).

With a house group

1. Before reading the first passage, ask half the group to identify with the Pharisee and the other half with the woman. Give some background to the attitude of the Pharisee to help them to do this (paragraph 1 above).

2. After reading Luke 7.36–50, divide into two groups (Pharisee and woman) and share your feelings about what happened.

3. Come together into one group. Why was the Pharisee unable to receive Jesus? What was the woman's strength?

4. Follow the study of Matthew 10.5-14 and 40–42 as outlined above and discuss the questions.

NB. Try not to allow the discussion to wander off on to other interesting issues thrown up by this passage. Your aim should be to bring the two passages together and consider the underlying significance of welcome or lack of welcome and to show that without welcome, mission is ineffectual.

ii Converting the church

Mark 10.13–52

Read and reflect on verses 13–16. The theme is again receptivity. Children can often see truths to which the rest of us are blind.

Read verses 17–31. Unlike the Pharisee, this man came with an open mind and actually 'heard' what Jesus was saying, but did not have the will to 'let go'. Had he done so, his life would have been immeasurably enriched by a whole new field of relationships (verses 29–31) and he would have discovered new depths of insight through fellowship with the poor. How much do we resemble this man?

Read verses 32–45. Notice the number of times in this chapter that Mark reminds us that Jesus is 'on the way', 'on the road. . .' and that others are following 'in the way'. There is a sense of movement and going forward. But the disciples were preoccupied with structure, power and status—things that would be static. They wanted a hierarchical organization (verse 37), to be in control, as they had been in organizing the distribution of food at the feeding of the five thousand. But Jesus, brushing aside all thoughts of 'upward mobility', talked about climbing down to serve with the poor and weak and hidden.

● We often talk in despair about 'the same small group of people left to do everything in church'. Could it be our fault? Is it due to our love of power, of being in control? Look again at the work of David Sharland (pages 17–18), Adrian Hopkins (page 34) and Magali Cunha (page 90), where whole communities are involved. What can we learn from their experience? How can we encourage wider participation?

● How can we become the 'servant church'? Reflect on this question in relation to the experiences of Magali Cunha in Brazil (pages 88–9).

● How can we, the body of Christ, begin 'to pray within the community instead of in the church' (page 93)?

● Are we too preoccupied with filling churches rather than 'going to people in their struggle'? (page 90) To what extent have we neglected Jesus' teaching about the Kingdom?

● Stephen Barton believes that the Protestant churches in Britain have dissipated energy in arguing whether the need is to proclaim the evangelical or social gospel and neglected the 'priesthood of all believers'. What should be distinctive about the church? How can we discover greater confidence in prayer and in God?

● Think of ways in which we can help people in Britain (including church members) to overcome their sense of 'British superiority' and become more open to learn from people of other cultures (page 109). What would it mean to receive the gospel from the poor? (page 48)

Read verses 46–52. When the gospel writers talk about sight and hearing they seem to imply also perceptiveness. There is a hint of this here, and so Bartimaeus 'followed' Jesus on the road (of discipleship?), no longer dependent on charity, but able to work and serve in the community. Like the woman in the house of Simon the Pharisee, who recognized her guilt, so Bartimaeus admitted his blindness, unlike the disciples who failed to see where Jesus was leading them. We too are blind until Jesus opens our eyes!

● What new insights have come to you through the stories in this book? How can you share them with others and work together for change?

With a house group

Before you read the first story, divide into two groups. Ask one group to identify with the mothers and the other with the disciples. After reading the story, share your reactions and insights together. Then continue with the rest of the study as outlined above.

iii Sharing the struggle

Read **Acts 16.16–24**. Paul's action at Philippi had far-reaching consequences—political detention on an unsubstantiated charge of practising illegal customs. Paul had attacked the cause of the girl's misery—the merciless exploitation of her psychic powers for financial gain. It was a matter of justice for the poor and defenceless. Child labour, including child prostitution, has still not been eradicated worldwide. To find out more information, consult your local library and/ or write to Unicef. Make a list of other evils we should be tackling.

Read **Mark 3.22–30**. Jesus declared that citizens of the Kingdom will always be in conflict against evil, in whatever shape or form (verses 22–27). He adds a serious reminder that there is no forgiveness for those who recognize its basic principles and then, opting for something less, stubbornly try to justify their self-interest and prejudice over against practical love and mercy.

● 'Christians who persist in their racial, sexual, or other kind of prejudice, have not finished being converted.' *(Third Latin American Congress on Evangelization in Quito, Ecuador 1992)* In what ways are we in the church blocking God's mission of reconciliation to the world?

Read **Mark 11.15–19.** Jesus himself engaged in non-violent protest on behalf of voiceless peasants cheated even in the holy Temple.

● Try to identify with Jane Montenegro's anger (page 93) coming from poverty in Asia to the affluence of Britain and her question: 'Where is God in all this?'
● What are we going to do about the gross injustice of world trade today? (For more information about this issue write to Christian Aid or CAFOD).

Although most countries in the South have formally put an end to their colonization, they are trapped in a vicious gridlock of domination and control worse than during colonial times. Events of the past still cast menacing shadows over contemporary events.

Our new conquistadores are the International Monetary Fund (IMF) through its Structural Adjustment Programme meant in theory to rescue Third World economies. The conventional prescription the IMF gives Third World countries includes devaluing the local currency and producing more for export. The drawback of this involves shortage of land for local food production, frenzied production by several countries of the same commodities, causing a glut and consequently a slump in commodity prices. Entangled in this vicious cycle it becomes necessary to give the Third World countries aid. The whole aid concept is a distortion of reality—the North gives aid

but with a string of conditions—(more control over the
destiny of the South); the North receives far more from
the South over and above what it gives in so-called aid. . .
(Moussa Conteh in *A Southern Perspective*, a paper for
Christian Aid)

● In the light of this, reflect again on Luke 4.16–19, remem-
bering that the 'year of the Lord's favour' refers to the year
of Jubilee when the debts of the poor were to be cancelled.
● How can we respond to the challenge put by Monica
Jones on page 28 about aid and the arms trade?
● Reflecting on Sydney Bailey's experiences in political
mediation (pages 100–105), how can we become more effective mediators of peace in our local communities?

With a house group

*Follow the suggestions outlined above. Together, write a letter to
your MP expressing your concern about the injustice of present
world trade patterns and requesting an increase in government
aid.*

*To find out more about ways to become involved in protest
against the arms trade write to Campaign against the Arms Trade
(see Appendix).*

---

iv Many faiths—one world

Read **Luke 7.1–10** trying to identify with

● **the Roman centurion**, whose religion included respect
for a number of gods—an ethos very different from that of
Palestine. There were no 'touching points', or so it seemed.
Yet he had an open mind and behaved with respect towards
the indigenous religion. Despite the prejudices of other
Romans towards Palestine, he had come to know some very
devout Jews and wanted to build them a synagogue.
● **the disciples and other Jewish onlookers**, who had been
strictly brought up to worship one God with complete

loyalty and whose tradition of 'holiness' (separateness) appeared to make it difficult for them to eat with or mix with people of other cultures. They appreciated his friendly approach but would have been cautious about the relationship.

● How would each of them react to Jesus' comment? What indication does this give to how Jesus might respond in an inter-faith situation today?

Read **Matthew 28.19**. Reflect on the word 'disciple', which implies 'learning from' rather than 'conversion to'. In the light of the experiences of Ivy Gutridge and Elizabeth Harris, was Jesus suggesting that we invite people of other faiths and those of no faith to 'learn' from him? And how different would this interpretation be to the way in which you have been conditioned to read this text?

● Read **Genesis 1.27** and **31**. What do these verses say about people born as Hindus in India, as Buddhists in Sri Lanka or as Muslims in Palestine?

● Read **Matthew 5.17–20**. This was Jesus' attitude to the teaching of Judaism. Make a list of other ways in which Jesus showed his respect for Judaism. What might he have said if he had been born in a Buddhist, Hindu, or Islamic culture?

● Read **Luke 24.28–29**. Notice that Jesus did not force his presence, but 'made as though he would continue his journey'.

● Read **John 16.13** and reflect on its meaning for today.

● Use Jane Montenegro's idea of lighting a candle as a focus for your reflections and follow her suggestions for breathing out negative feelings (page 98).

● What challenge does all this make to us in the Decade of Evangelism? Consider Nick Drayson's experience (page 54) and that of Ivy Gutridge (pages 111–12) and how we evangelize through 'friendship'.

Build on this study by getting to know a person, or family from another faith, and begin to discover what they believe and practise. Ask them to take you to their place of worship.

We are to build friendships out of love and for their own sake—as bridges of understanding. But do not befriend to convert. In God's time, not ours, the Spirit of God will do whatever converting may be necessary and that may need to happen as much within ourselves as in others!

With a house group

Begin by dividing into two groups to identify with the centurion or Jewish onlookers. Stay in these groups to share your feelings and then come together and follow the questions and readings as above. Follow up your study by inviting someone of another faith to come and speak to you and take you to a place of worship.

Holy Spirit,
cooling and refreshing breeze,
moving within us
as you first moved
on the face of the waters,
fill us and refresh us
with your all-pervading presence.

Holy Spirit,
fire of God,
burning within the hearts of prophets
until they cry out against injustice,
cleanse us of insularity
and reluctance to protest when evil prospers.

Holy Spirit —
rushing wind,
unconfined,
blowing where you will across the world,
sweeping us up with your power,
raging,
buffeting,
causing havoc,
uprooting what has stood for centuries,
pulling us on,
turning us inside out with new insights,
preventing us from standing still,
leading us into all truth,
impelling us to move with you
across all boundaries
bringing peace, unity and reconciliation —
empower and renew us
and do not allow us
to resist your direction.

Appendix:
Abbreviations and addresses

AIDS	Acquired immune deficiency syndrome
CBT	Communidad Biblica Teologica
CSI	Church of South India
FMLN	Farabundo Marti National Liberation Front
GNB	Good News Bible
MCZ	Methodist Church Zimbabwe
MP	Member of Parliament
NGO	non-governmental organization
NIV	New International Version
NJB	New Jerusalem Bible
PEN	Philippine Ecumenical Network
REB	Revised English Bible
SAN	the health and literacy programme of the Baptist Association in San Salvador
SEN	State Enrolled Nurse
UCJGCI	United Church in Jamaica and the Cayman Islands
UK	United Kingdom
UN	United Nations
UNHCR	United Nations High Commission for Refugees
Unicef	United Nations (International) Children's (Emergency) Fund
VSO	Voluntary Service Overseas
WCRP	World Conference on Religion and Peace
WHO	World Health Organization
WIFG	Wolverhampton Inter-Faith Group
YMCA	Young Men's Christian Association
YWCA	Young Women's Christian Association

Amity Foundation
Overseas Co-ordination Office
4 Jordan Road
Kowloon
Hong Kong

Baptist Missionary Society
Baptist House
129 Broadway
Didcot
Oxon
OX11 8RT

Campaign against the Arms Trade
11 Goodwin Street
London N4

CAFOD (Catholic Fund for Overseas Development)
2 Romero Close
Stockwell Road
London
SW9 9TY

Council of Churches for Britain and Ireland
Inter-Church House
35-41 Lower Marsh
London
SE1 7RL

Christian Aid
Inter-Church House
35-41 Lower Marsh
London
SE1 7RL

Christians Abroad
Stockwell Green
London
SW9 9HP

Christians Aware
10 Springfield Road
Leicester
LE2 3BD

Church Missionary Society
Partnership House
157 Waterloo Road
London
SE1 8UU

Council for World Mission
Livingstone House
11 Carteret Street
London
SW1H 9DL

Bridges of the Spirit

Grassroots
Luton Industrial College
Chapel Street
Luton
Beds
LU1 2SE

Methodist Church Overseas Division
25 Marylebone Road
London
NW1 5JR

National Missionary Council of England and Wales
Mission Secretariat
Holcombe House
The Ridgeway
London
NW7 4HY

Quaker Peace and Service
Friends' House
Euston Road
London
NW1 2BJ

South American Missionary Society
Allen Gardiner House
Pembury Road
Tunbridge Wells
Kent
TN2 3QU

United Society for the Propagation of the Gospel
Partnership House
157 Waterloo Road
London
SE1 8UU

World Council of Churches
150 Route de Ferney
1211 Geneva 2
Switzerland